Rebuilding After Divorce

Making Your House a Home Again

Rebuilding After Divorce

Making Your House a Home Again

Rose Sweet

Saint Benedict Press
Charlotte, North Carolina

ISBN: 978-1-935302-65-0

Cover design by Christopher J. Pelicano

Printed and bound in the United States of America.

Saint Benedict Press
Charlotte, North Carolina
2012

O Lord, I love the habitation of thy house,
and the place where thy glory dwells.

— Psalm 26:8

Table of Contents

Introduction The Rejection of Divorce ix

Part 1: Get ready to rebuild

1. See Your Life as a House 3
2. Get Ready to Relocate 11
3. Face the Move Head-on 21
4. Let God Lead You 31
5. Let Your Father Be Your Architect . . . 41
6. Enjoy Making Plans 55
7. Lay a Firm Foundation 67
8. Work from God's Blueprints 79
9. Expect an Adequate Timeframe 89
10. Don't Rush the Process 99
11. Clear Your Title 109
12. Erect Sturdy Boundaries 127
13. Build a Solid Roof 145

Part 2: Make your house a home

14.	Clear Out Your Closets	155
15.	Stock Up Your Kitchen	173
16.	Make Your Bedroom Special	181
17.	Keep Up on Your Cleaning	193
18.	Don't Hide Things in the Cellar . . .	203
19.	Learn to Love Your Laundry Room	215
20.	Make the Kids' Room Safe	237
21.	Enjoy Your Living Room	257
22.	Equip Your Garage	269
23.	Gather Around the Fireplace	283
24.	Look Forward to the Best	289
Epilogue	The Best Is Yet to Come	285
Notes	. . . .	303

Introduction

The Rejection of Divorce

THE child picked last by his playmates for the team, the suitor whose proposal is rejected, and the spouse left at home while the other walks out the door for the last time—all are sharing in some sense in the tragic rejection of Jesus, who was, and still is, the most rejected of all. Scripture tells us "He was despised and rejected by men, a man of sorrows, and acquainted with grief."[1] Jesus wanted only the best for mankind, and yet there was no room for Him at the inn, no place to lay His head, and seemingly only a splintered cross for Him in the end. But we know that was *not* the end, and your divorce is not the end for you either—even though sometimes it certainly may feel that way.

This book is about rebuilding your life, turning your house back into a real home, even when your hopes and dreams have been terribly splintered. I've written other books for those who are recently separated, newly divorced, or still raw with emotion (*A Woman's Guide to Healing the Heartbreak of Divorce*[2] and *Healing the Divorced Heart*[3]) which I suggest you read first. There's no point trying to rebuild your life when you're still emotionally exhausted and gushing emotional blood. With this book, I want to pick up at a place past those initial shock waves and help point you to a promising future. I want *you* to be able to pack up your bags, as it were, and like the Israelites head out to a new and joyful "land of milk and honey." When you get there, you'll be able to lay a new foundation, build a beautiful home, and enjoy life again. But how do you get there? How can you create a home that shelters you from the torrential rains and earthquakes of life?

Jesus is our hope

Jesus is the only one who gives you and me the fullest and most perfect hope. But those can seem to be

> Many divorced men and women have the tendency to rebuild around their finances and new relationships in a desperate attempt to recover all the things that were lost.

just nice Christian words that we have trouble really believing. Instead of trusting God as they ought, many divorced men and women have the tendency to rebuild around their finances and new relationships in a desperate attempt to recover all the things that were lost. But these are not the most important things—rebuilding your life must begin with the firm "foundation," not the interior decorating. Scripture tells us Jesus is the "cornerstone" of all creation. He's not just a biblical character from long ago floating somewhere up in the sky—He's real. We have to "build" on Him because we come from Him, we were created to return to Him, and He alone knows how to give us the life and love we seek.

Sadly, many people know *about* Jesus, but they do not know Him. And how can you trust someone you don't really know very well? In this book I want to introduce you to Christ in a way that reaches your head and your heart—perhaps in a slightly different perspective than before—by sharing some of the "blueprints" for life that He's given us in Sacred Scripture. I'll talk later about getting your finances back in order, making the kids happy, or finding a new love, but first things first: *your foundation in Christ.*

Jesus knows about rejection and the death of divorce, and He promises you new life in Him. He is the "cornerstone" that was so violently rejected by the "builders" (those who were supposedly the architects of the Jewish community) and then rose from the place of death to return in shining glory to show us the way to our true home. The rejection of divorce has probably toppled your life and shaken your very foundation.

Have hope! In building on Him, which is a union of sorts with Him, know that there is life after death and a resurrection waiting for *you*.

Part 1

Get Ready to Rebuild

When I think about building and moving into a new home, I just want to concentrate on my color scheme, the decorations, and where I want to put my Christmas tree. But the realtor, lender, architect, engineer, building inspector, plumber, electrician, carpenter, and oh so many more have other ideas. I hate to think about it, but there's just so much that has to be done first!

—*Nancy W., Ohio*

Chapter 1

See Your Life as a House

ONE day I discovered I had a large family of rats living inside the space in my house between the ceiling and the roof. I was washing my face at my bathroom sink and heard them at first—scurrying overhead—and eventually smelled the musky odor of their wet fur and urine coming out of a ceiling vent overhead. It was disgusting! I knew I needed help to get into those dark, creepy places where the problem lived. I called the Truly Nolen pest control company, who sent Hugo, their rat specialist. Hugo climbed up on the roof and saw that several vents had never been covered from the time the house had been built, over twenty-five years before. Whole families of rodents had crawled in and made their home in *my* home! I paid Hugo nine hundred dollars to seal the vents, set traps, and then come every few days to clear out the dead carcasses until they were all gone. Thankfully, Hugo sprayed a fresh, pine-scented deodorizer into the space every few days to cover the stench. It made the whole house smell sweet and clean, but what a price to pay for room freshener!

This is one of many true stories in my life that I've used to illustrate principles about rebuilding your life after divorce. My history of attempted marriages and divorce is not pretty—I've been civilly divorced three times, a fact that still saddens me. Coming into my young adulthood in the 1960s, I had a lot of open vents in my life and "rats" of ignorance, pride, and fear had been making nests there for a long time. The first time I attempted marriage, I was quite young and naïve, under grave pressure to escape my childhood home, and only legally married for nine months to an alcoholic who took his fists to me. I escaped one night and came back home, and my parents helped me file for a Decree of Nullity (annulment) in our local diocese. Back then it was a public shame to be in therapy, I had no wise counsel, and I didn't really learn from my mistake. I soon tried marriage again, still not with the right intent and in violation of that which the Church teaches about marriage. How can a valid marriage bond be formed when one or both of you don't really understand what the Church teaches or what you are really doing? When that's the case, all you *can* do is try.

This attempt at marriage ended quickly, and I received another annulment. This time the Church said (for Pete's sake) to *get counseling*. My third try was a frantic attempt to have children before it was too late and

I was too old. I married outside the Catholic Church for a third time; having no idea the relationship was doomed from the start. During that time I finally came back to my senses and my faith. My pastor helped me file a third annulment (a Lack of Form), and I entered a period of healing and maturity that was long past due.

But the feelings of rejection, the shame and shock of being divorced, and having to face life on my own once again remain clear memories. Shortly after my third attempt at wedded bliss, I knew something was very wrong—with me!—and I finally called out to God for help. Although the marriage ended, my new relationship with God was just beginning, and He has remained with me through all the ups and downs ever since.

Don't think you know it all

When you're sick and start taking antibiotics, you eventually start to feel better, but you're still not well. You get out of bed too soon. You go outside and wear yourself down and end up in bed again in a few days, feeling worse than ever. That's a picture of what happened to me as I began to get some spiritual health. I'd turned my life over to God, was taking His antibiotics, and was feeling much better. I got anxious about wanting to go back outside and "play." But full recovery takes a long time. God has a lot of work to do in each of us.

So after the initial shock of my last divorce and a

short period of readjustment, I started to think, *Okay, I know I need healing time. Maybe two to three years at most. I can do that. Then I will be ready to marry again. Yes, I will be good and ready.*

But in year three there was no hope in sight.

Year five came and went, and I began to panic.

In year seven, something happened. The closer I continued to draw to Him, the more honest I could be about facing how damaged I'd been. Seeing I was finally ready, God gently but firmly reached into my chest, grabbed my heart, and pulled it into His. I'd rediscovered both the God and Church of my youth as a cradle Catholic growing up in the 1950s. And now I was at a place where I could quit looking out the front door to see who may be walking up the steps and begin to rest in my relationship with God.

That surprised me because the last thing I ever wanted to turn into was a single, old "Church lady." But here I was, often listening to Christian radio instead of just my favorite stations , going to daily Mass, frequenting the Sacraments, and discovering beautiful prayers and traditions of the Church—some that I had forgotten since childhood. I was changing, not out of fear or duty but because I wanted to! I had finally started surrendering my heart to God, and He was faithfully filling those empty places in my heart.

For close to two decades I've also been in divorce ministry, helping others to get though their pain. I'm the oldest of a large Catholic family, and by my natural temperament I have the "gift" of taking charge of others and telling them what to do! Yes, I have learned some humility—the hard way. Those of us who are called to be "wounded healers" continue our own healing the more we humbly and unselfishly reach out to others. So I've asked many of those divorced men and women who have been in my groups or seminars to share with you in this book how they rebuilt after divorce. They have their own "rat" stories, and one woman shares about being plagued by the "pit bulls" in her life. If you have the eyes to see and ears to hear, you'll find God's blueprints for healing in these and other normal, day-to-day situations.

Take time to seal the vents

Like my house with unsealed roof vents, some marriages fail because some significant holes had been open from the beginning and—in a certain sense—vermin were already living in the mind and heart. Maybe it is grave immaturity, gross selfishness, or addictive thoughts and behaviors. These sins are not sterile. They multiply and grow and take over the attic in our heads, and they cause an offensive stink that affects everyone in the family. Ultimately we have to endure a time-consuming clean-up process, and—as you who are divorced know—there's a huge price to pay; a lot more than Hugo's nine hundred dollars.

When you're rebuilding after divorce, you'll first have to stop, take stock of what is going on, prioritize what needs to be done, get some professional help if necessary, and then make a specific plan of action. Maybe you've already done some of that reconstruction.

The temptation will be to avoid the pain—or the hard work—and rush through the process or ignore the little clicking sounds of rat feet overhead. Every divorced person I've talked to who rushed into new relationships or plunged head-first into something good or valuable that easily became a distraction (like parenting or work), ended up deeply injuring themselves again and regretting it. They admit they didn't listen; they thought they knew it all. "I thought I wasn't like those other people—I was smarter!" When I hear such comments, we laugh together. We understand each other because I used to think like that too.

I want to help you rebuild a beautiful, rich, and satisfying life. I want your house—wherever it is—to

> When you're rebuilding after divorce, you'll first have to stop, take stock of what is going on, prioritize what needs to be done, get some professional help if necessary, and then make a specific plan of action.

become a vibrant home filled with life and love. But trust me, there's no rushing the restoration of your life or the sealing of your open vents. It takes time to do it right. You do not want to go through divorce again, do you?

Chapter 2

Get Ready to Relocate

DIVORCE means you have to "move"—even if you *don't* have to move. You may stay in the same house. But your life will be changed forever, and—if you haven't already—you'll be moving into new and unexpected territory. If you get overwhelmed or anxious about having to leave one life behind and go into another, remember you're not the only one who's ever had to relocate and rebuild.

Let me take you back to the very first book of the Bible, Genesis, where we'll find the story of Adam and Eve and the first divorce—and forced relocation—in the visible world. The powerful truths in their tale are still relevant today. The couple was in a loving union with God, but tragically they chose to be unfaithful to Him, leaving Him, as it were, for someone else. It was Satan who successfully seduced Adam and Eve, and then God's justice demanded they pack up their bags and move. Do you recall this Old Testament story? Let's visit the Garden of Eden.

Adam and Eve had it all

If you're reading your Bible, you'll see that in Genesis 1:3 Adam was at first by himself, the only human in creation at that point, and God decided it was not good for him to be alone. I used to think that meant everyone had to be married to be happy, but I found through further study that wasn't the case—there are a lot of us who never marry who are quite happy. Marriage, as God intended it, is one rich and beautiful way to live, but it's not the only way. Since we're made in the image of God and God is a "communion" of Persons who perfectly love each other, we need to give and receive authentic love to another to become our true self. The Persons of the Holy Trinity make perfect, perpetual gifts of themselves to each other. When we learn to live as best we can in that same self-giving way—wanting only the best for others, no matter who they are—we find that it is good. It's good to give authentic love and good to *receive* it.

So God gave Adam the gift of Eve. Her gift was Adam. Before they sinned, they were both completely open to God and saturated to overflowing with His love, and they poured that love out like honey onto each other. We can surmise that if sin had not yet entered their hearts that they must have been pure and holy . . . and perfectly happy! But, darn it all, it lasted only a few short Bible verses.

Adam and Eve had everything they could ever want

in the Garden of Eden—love, comfort, pleasure, a sense of belonging, and perfect security. God gave them an abundance of choices for food, with the exception of the one tree in the middle of the garden. It was the tree of the Knowledge of Good and Evil. "Don't touch," God had said, "or you'll die." We don't know exactly what they understood at that point, but I'm guessing that God made it pretty clear that death was *not* a good thing.

Satan hated the fact that God deeply loved mankind and had a special plan for man. Hate begat a desire in his black heart for the death of all of us. So the enemy slithered into their home and pointed right to the forbidden fruit, luring Adam and Eve into thinking they should be able to have whatever they wanted. He oh-so-subtly suggested that perhaps God was not to be trusted; that He was withholding something good from them. Scripture also tells us that Satan suggested they could even be *like* God—determining for themselves what was right and wrong. Their sin was believing those lies and focusing first on what else might satisfy them besides what God had already given them. They began to doubt that God was indeed a loving Father. That's at the root of our sins too.

Adam and Eve divorce God

In Adam and Eve's turning away from God, the first human divorce happened. Even though she didn't go down to the courthouse and file separation papers, Eve spiritually left God in choosing her way over His. But where was Adam? Standing passively as his wife was being charmed, deceived, and seduced into death? Was he trying not to make waves? Afraid of her yelling at him? Was the enemy too confusing, scary, or overwhelming for him? Why didn't he grab her arm, shout "NO!" and remind his wife of God's goodness? In his cowardice—for whatever reason—he failed to protect her and thereby abandoned her (another form of divorce). Then, when he joined his wife in the sin of greedily grasping for what they were told not to touch, the divorce was complete. Adam and Eve had now cut themselves off from the grace of God.

> In that sin man *preferred* himself to God and by that very act scorned him . . . seduced by the devil, he wanted to "be like God" but "without God, before God, and not in accordance with God."
>
> — CCC 398

The Catechism of the Catholic Church says:

In that sin man *preferred* himself to God and by that very act scorned him . . . seduced by the devil, he wanted to "be like God" but "without God, before God, and not in accordance with God."

—*CCC* 398

Adam and Eve get evicted

Although God loved the first couple, He doesn't tolerate the stench of sin. Perfect justice demands that a price be paid for scorning Almighty God, a price Adam and Eve could never pay. Their rejection of Him and all that He had given them was just too great, so Adam and Eve were quickly evicted from their gorgeous garden home. There was no thirty-day notice; the angel of the Lord came with a fiery sword and drove them out into the wilderness. Clang! The gates of paradise were locked.

Can you imagine how it must have felt to be kicked out of your home like that? And to have lost the rich inheritance that was supposed to be passed on to your children? Our first parents, Adam and Eve, passed on their sin and death to us. If you've been divorced, you know the consequences that get dumped on the children too.

But Adam and Eve still had the most important thing God had ever given them: Himself. They still had the faithful and enduring love of a Father who, despite their sinful choices and their required eviction, immediately promised to bring them home again someday.

God demands perfect justice, but at the same time He drenches us in His perfect mercy: there *was* one who could pay the price levied on humanity—God Himself—and He promised to come and make things right some day. But only when mankind was ready to understand.

> God demands perfect justice, but at the same time He drenches us in His perfect mercy.

"I will put enmity between you and the woman, and between your seed and her seed; he shall bruise your head, and you shall bruise his heel."

—Genesis 3:15

This short verse is GOOD NEWS! It foretells the undoing of all of Adam and Eve's mess. It speaks of the arrival of "the woman" (Mary) who will fight against Satan; she'll bear "seed" to crush sin and death and restore us to God and His paradise. From the Father, through Mary, the conquering hero (Jesus the Savior) is promised to come to satisfy the debt our parents incurred. This is the story of creation, our fall, and our redemption—and it's so central to humanity that the theme recurs throughout history, art, literature, and even our children's fables. It's the essence of our Catholic faith, and—in a certain sense—you could say that Jesus the God-Man would rescue His Bride and bring the happily-ever-after to this fairy tale gone bad.

A new Adam and Eve

Maybe you'd like to know why I'm sharing so much about this old Bible story to an audience of divorced men and women? Simple—*this is the story of every divorce*. Unless we understand what really happened then, we will be doomed to repeat it again. You'll either go through life like the same old Adam and Eve, whose sinful nature we inherited, or you can become like the new Adam and Eve who knew how to build a home filled with life and love.

The *old Eve* said no to God.

The *new Eve* is Mary, who shows us how to say "Yes! Let it be done to me according to Thy Word." Your new life must be one that is open and receptive to God's will and thus His many blessings of life and love. It must be a new life of yes, yes, YES to God.

The *old Adam* was a selfish, quiet coward who let his wife go to her death.

The *new Adam* is Jesus. His Bride is the Church (us), and He courageously gave up His life to save us. Your new life must be one where you are willing to die to selfishness in any form, or you will never build that home you so desire.

The choice is yours.

But don't worry. Just like Adam and Eve, *you* still have God's love and His promise of salvation.

Your real home is Heaven

Last year I went with a group of friends and family for a week at a waterfront home in Stinson Beach, California. I wasn't too excited about the location because during June the weather consists of thick, cold fog all day long. But I imagined an adorable little beach cottage where I could snuggle up in front of a fire, cook a nice meal, and read a good book.

Sadly, my friends had waited until the last minute to rent a house, and the only thing the realtor had left was the oldest, run-down shack on the block. The paint was chipping inside and out, the floors creaked, the kitchen was dark, and all the rooms had that funny, dank smell that no one wants to admit is mold.

I took a look around and thought *Ugh-h-h*! But then I did what I always do—complain a bit and then try to make the best of it. I found a few old jelly glasses in the kitchen, cut some greenery outside with a rusty kitchen knife, and put my little vases around the house. I rummaged through drawers and found some white votive candles that I put on the patio and in the living room. I fluffed up the pillows and turned down the beds like they do in hotels and put on some music. Finally, I opened up the windows for some fresh, sea air, and then I put my hands on my hips, surveying the surroundings with great satisfaction. The smell was still bad, but I felt better.

That night we had friends over for a barbecue, and when they walked in the first thing my girlfriend said was, "What a dump! And what is that smell?"

Argh-h-h-h! Did she have to remind me? I laughed and agreed it was a dump, and then I reminded myself that it was only temporary. This was not my real home, and soon I would be in my beautiful, comfortable surroundings again.

This life is not our home

I'm in that home now, writing this book, and I've decided to use the analogy of having to move out of a house after divorce or rebuild a physical home as the basis for rebuilding your life. A warm and cozy home has always brought me a sense of security, peace, and joy, and I bet it has for you too. But divorce breaks up the home, robs us of peace, and utterly kills our joy. Like the old beach house I endured for a week, divorce stinks.

But this earthly life—and, specifically, this painful period after divorce—is only temporary. This life is not our home. Heaven is our destiny, our true home.

What does Jesus tell us?

> "Let not your hearts be troubled; believe in God, believe also in me. In my Father's house are many rooms; if it were not so, would I have told you that I go to prepare a place for you?

> And when I go and prepare a place for you, I will come again and will take you to myself, that where I am you may be also. And you know the way where I am going."
>
> —John 14:1–4

I want this book to help you find your way back "home" after a divorce, like I did. Do you know the way to do that?

> Thomas said to him, "Lord, we do not know where you are going; how can we know the way?" Jesus said to him, "I am the way, and the truth, and the life; no one comes to the Father, but by me.
>
> —John 14:5–6

Chapter 3

Face the Move Head-on

WHERE were you on September 11, 2001? After digesting the horrifying news splashed all over television networks or playing from car radios, most of the nation moved quickly from disbelief into varying degrees of mourning. Special news stories celebrating the lives of the victims who died played continuously.

But the daily details of life can be distracting—even from a terrible tragedy. A funny thing about people in shock is that they don't always walk around with eyes wide open and mouths open, aghast. They don't always freeze up or appear catatonic, as we might expect. People in shock more often seem normal, busily going about their lives. After the news about the Twin Towers tragedy broke, some people finished their coffee and went back to work, apparently untouched. Were they unfeeling? No. Many were simply still in shock and functioning on autopilot as a way to deal with the blow.

Don't some of us do that after a divorce? The reality that our life is about to change and we are going to have to build a new life can be overwhelming. We try to avoid the pain we know is coming by keeping ourselves distracted and busy with life: the kids, the house, the job, maybe even some ridiculously unimportant project or hobby that preoccupies much of our time. Shock can be a numb place that feels safer than going outside to look at the collapsing towers of our life.

> The reality that our life is about to change and we are going to have to build a new life can be overwhelming.

Others may face the trauma squarely but then, after a while, go into shock when they finally catch up with themselves. Regardless of how one reacts after divorce, everyone is going to have to face the reality and the depth of what has happened and what needs to be done.

Using your heart and your head together

One of the cultural problems today is that we tend to "think" with our feelings, giving our fleeting, fickle, and out-of-control emotions priority over our intellect. The timeless wisdom of the Church teaches us that feelings—while normal—are always to be subject to our intellect and will. *That means your head should take charge over your heart.* So even if you feel like this is the end of the world, you can begin to calm and center yourself by thinking of what is real:

- ◇ It *feels* like the end of the world, but I *know* it is not.
- ◇ It *feels* like God is nowhere to be found, but I *know* He's right here.
- ◇ It *feels* like I'll never be happy again, but I *know* that's not true.

Here's an email I received from a divorced woman who in her head wants to trust God, but because she is so used to allowing her emotions to drive her (while her intellect, logic, faith, and will take a back seat), she can't get there:

> I went to confession yesterday, telling the priest, "I am sorry for being angry and taking it out on everyone else lately and for such a lack of trust, faith, and hope in God." Father told me to try: TRY to think of a few things every day that you're blessed with and TRY to put the uncontrolled in God's hands. I have said that a million times to myself! But saying and doing it is my problem! I want to put my cares and worries in His hands. But I never seemed to be able to let go.

The emotions will always fight for control. That's part of our inheritance from Adam and Eve, who *felt* like they could not trust God and who *felt* like eating that danged fruit and did!

Barb shared with me how she let God reshape her feelings about Him with the facts of who He really is:

> I had followed everything I'd been taught about God, all the rules, commandments, etc., ad nauseum. As a result, [after the divorce] my life was hell and my kids' well-being was threatened. I very honestly said, "@#$% you, God, and the horse you rode in on . . . except for baby Jesus." LOL. The false God I had constructed was in a million broken pieces all over the floor, and I didn't have the willingness or energy to pick them up and put them back together. Someone brilliantly suggested I LET GOD put Himself back together in my life. So, I did—and He did!

You might be stuck *feeling* that your future is going to be terrible, or you may be *feeling* happy and excited about a new future and think it's all going to be wonderful. Or you may *feel* God has abandoned you or *feel* that He's going to bring you everything you want. Instead of allowing your emotions to take you to these polarized extremes, let's have a little reality check about what to expect during the rebuilding time after a divorce.

The passing of time will not fix the problems

You might be feeling better than you did when the divorce was new. Time has a way of allowing us to get used to pain and problems, but the root causes of a divorce do not get fixed without intentionally addressing them. If it's been a while since your family fell apart and you feel better, remember that doesn't necessarily mean there has been full healing or that you are really ready to move on. After reading this book and making a specific plan for rebuilding, you can begin to use your time more wisely. I'll help you.

Panic and fear can tear down your house

Judy wrote to me,

When my husband and I separated, I was forced to move along with my daughter into a residence of my own. Not having worked for twenty years and lacking self-confidence, I remember great waves of fear washing over me. Having little in the way of financial support (actually zero) and knowing I was totally responsible for supporting myself and my daughter for the first time in my life, I was completely consumed with worry and dread.

We won't have the energy to pack, move, or rebuild a new life when our energies are being consumed by fear and dread. Remember that fear is a feeling, and feelings come and go with changing circumstances. Don't ignore your fears, but learn to put more trust in your faith in God than in your fear.

Old wounds may reappear

Have you ever peeled wallpaper off a wall and found layers of different papers beneath? Everyone—divorced or not—has past emotional wounds that may have remained buried or unhealed during their marriages. I'm not saying we all need to run down to the therapist, but you can understand that traumas like divorce have a way of ripping off all the layers and exposing old stuff. You'll need to expect that. It may make the rebuilding more difficult and maybe take a longer time, but with patience and grace God can make everything new.

Barb had a long childhood history of feeling neglected that reared its head when her husband abandoned her and her children. Her house and physical surroundings had substituted for the security she needed, and when she lost her home after divorce she wrote,

> My house was often more my "mother" than
> my mom was: warm, safe, smelled good, a place

to renew myself. Moving was always about losing my mother again.

Barb also shared the heartbreak of the stigma and shame that can come with divorce.

I hated uprooting the kids as a result of their dad having turned our lives upside down. But I was stubbornly bound and determined to make sure ours was a loving and emotionally well-balanced home. Even though we were now labeled a "broken family."

Some may be too emotionally distraught to think of "rebuilding"

Jeff sent me an email:

I know when I first started going through divorce that I initially felt that my life was over. I felt like all the years I spent building my career, helping my wife through two very difficult pregnancies, and building what I thought was a wonderful family life for my kids was suddenly being thrown down the drain. The emotional burden from all of this left me feeling physically exhausted. I'm a hiker, and I didn't have energy to take hikes or even think about having fun. Sometimes it felt like it was all I could do just to keep breathing. There were literally some moments when I felt like I could have a heart attack. But much of this is purely emotions running their course. And, over time, the storm will pass.

Seek God immediately and He'll throw you a lifeline

You'll need more than a lifeline to rebuild a life, but it's a beginning!

God is with the divorced person at every stage of rebuilding, even when one doesn't believe or can't feel His presence. Patricia is one of the "stars" on *The Catholic's Divorce Survival Guide* DVD series I produced. She was divorced by her husband, went through the annulment process, and returned after many years to a full sacramental life. You can hear some of her story on the DVD series, but she emailed the longer version to me:

> My husband served me with divorce. There's a long story there and one which you, Rose, know very well (the story of the BBQ salesman in Show No. 1). My attorney told me that I could not leave the house. I had gotten to a place and point after living in our home for two months (following the serving) that I had become liter-

ally "a wreck." My husband would scream at me every day to "GET OUT, GET OUT," and I was trapped by my attorney's instructions. My husband had moved out of our bedroom and into the guest room. However, he would invade my room at all hours of the day and night. Walking through, doing this and that. All very calculated. I had not just started shaking—my whole body would convulse. I could not buy another home as it would then become community property. I was completely boxed in. But I called out to God for a lifeline. He heard me! Some dear friends called me and told me to go out, find a house. They would buy it, and I could rent it from them! Talk about a gift from God! . . . it was small, however, a good size for a now-single woman with two kitty cats, and it fit all of my needs. We had a thirty-day escrow, which was unheard of then. . . .

I had to keep things "quiet" about moving. I was "found out" the day before. My girlfriends came in and helped me pack my things. The mover came in the morning.

I remember that first night. I spun around this little house and was so delighted, so relieved! I climbed into bed that night with my two cats and NO ONE walked through the room in the middle of the night! I had my little house all to myself! It was so freeing! It was so delicious! Our Lord most certainly had His hand in this.

Remember, God *does* have His hand on your life, whether or not you feel like He does.

Chapter 4

Let God Lead You

God: "Moses. Moses."
Moses: "I am here, Lord."

Do you remember the scene of the burning bush in the 1956 movie *The Ten Commandments* with Charlton Heston starring as Moses? I was about ten years old when I first saw it and have watched it over the years with continued delight and inspiration. I highly recommend that you make some popcorn and have the whole family, even the teenagers, watch the show together. Don't let them complain about how old the film is; just enjoy the timeless story. It's long, so start watching early.

It's best first to read the story of Moses in Scripture, but movies—if faithful to God's Word—lend a beautiful dimension of sight and sound that engages the senses. In the Cecil B. DeMille epic, God speaks to Moses on Mount Sinai in a special-effects voice that is deep, sacred, and a little scary! The movie script follows pretty closely to the story in the book of Genesis, chapter 3:

God: Put off thy shoes from off thy feet, for the place thou standest is holy ground. I am the god of your fathers, the god of Abraham, the god of Isaac and the god of Jacob.

Moses: Lord . . . Lord, why do you not hear the cries of their children in the bondage of Egypt?

God: I have surely seen the affliction of my people which are in Egypt, and I have heard their cry by reason of their taskmasters, for I know their sorrows. Therefore, I will send thee, Moses, unto Pharaoh, that thou mayest bring my people out of Egypt.

Moses: Who am I, Lord, that you should send me? How can I lead this people out of bondage? What words can I speak that they will heed?

God: I will teach thee what thou wilt say. When thou hast brought forth the people, they shall serve me upon this mountain. I will put my laws into their hearts, and into their minds will I write them. Now, therefore, go and I will be with thee.

Moses: But if I say to your children that the god of their fathers has sent me, they will ask "What is his name?" How shall I answer them?

God: I am, that I am. Thou shalt say "I am" hath
        sent me unto you.[1]

In this epic of God leading the Israelites out of the
bondage of Egyptian slavery, there is a powerful message for divorced men and women. Maybe you have felt
like God has not seemed to hear the aching cries of
your heart or those of your children after a divorce. But
just as He told Moses, He *has* heard and He is going to
lead you out of the bondage of pain and loneliness after
your divorce.

God's people had been oppressed by the harsh rule
of an Egyptian pharaoh for hundreds of years. They
were miserable and constantly dreamed of and prayed
for deliverance. God never abandoned them, just as He
never abandons us. But, as a result of God permitting
(and protecting) the gift of our free will, all kinds of
trouble can occur. Some of us bring that trouble on ourselves; others of us get unfairly caught in the crossfire.
That's one of the ways that bad things happen to good
people, but we always have hope. If you were reading an
adventure novel and had just ended the chapter where
all the innocent people were captured or tortured, would
you put the book down and exclaim, "How unfair! They
did not deserve that! How could the author let this happen?" I think not. Instead, you'd keep reading, understanding that this is your favorite author, who in the end
always brings about a happy ending for the good guys.

In the story of our lives, God is the Author, and we can be certain that there will be a happy ending for the good guys (those who love Him and are called by Him).

That is the story of *your* life—but maybe right now you just don't know what the next chapter will hold. The Israelites' slavery was also not the end of their story. God remembered His promise to their forefathers and showed them the way to a new home, their Promised Land, "flowing with milk and honey." Will you read their story in Scripture? I hope so. It's in the Old Testament book of Exodus, which means a great, big MOVE out of Egypt!

Get ready, though, because the road to a new life will sometimes seem long. The Israelites had to leave their home in Egypt and wander through the hot, dry desert for forty years because they started complaining, got impatient, and didn't listen to God on the journey. With you, God may repeat the same ways of deliverance as He did with the Israelites, but don't you repeat the mistakes *they* made!

He'll send you a leader

Moses was chosen to liberate the people from slavery, out of the bondage to Pharaoh and into a new life of freedom in God. God prepared and instructed Moses for the job, and sometimes you'll need a Moses who has been instructed to help you. Look for those who can lead you to freedom and recovery: a loving parent, a good friend, a wise therapist, a holy priest, or a spiritual director. It may be a good author, an on-fire speaker, or, on a larger scale, the Church—our Mother—who is always here to show you the way home too.

Sometimes you will have to be the Moses for your own family, leading the unruly ex-slaves away from the things that have been familiar to them and into an unknown desert.

He'll only let you take some of your things with you

With almost no warning, the Israelites had to pack up and leave Egypt, and they had to travel lightly. No way could they drag all their things into the harsh desert environment. If they tried to carry it all, they'd be exhausted and maybe even dead trying to hang onto all their belongings in the hot, dry desert. There are things that have been in your life that God does not want you to take on the journey into the promised land of the new home He has for you. You might already have an idea of what those things are that you must leave behind.

He'll feed you along the way

Even though they were slaves, when the Israelites were in Egypt they could still access fresh meat and other foods that didn't grow out in the scorching, barren desert. Paying more attention to their appetites than their hearts, they started grumbling and even thinking they should turn back and stay in slavery rather than forge ahead to freedom. After divorce, it's sometimes common to want to go back to your old life because the unknown future is so difficult and scary. Unless you are working on reconciliation—and I pray that this may be a possibility for you—that old life is clearly not available any longer. It may not even be a safe place for you or your children. The Israelites complained about their plight because *they did not trust God to feed them.* In our human frailty we also fail to trust God (remember, that was Adam and Eve's first sin).

> After divorce, it's sometimes common to want to go back to your old life because the unknown future is so difficult and scary

But God did feed His people. He sent bread that came down from Heaven—manna. It was fresh every morning, but the people were forbidden to gather it up and store it for the next day. Do you know why? God was trying to teach them to quit hoarding out of fear that there would not be enough. He wanted them to start trusting Him to bring them what they needed every day. Don't we also hoard in certain areas, especially after having our things torn away by divorce? Remember that God *will* supply your basic needs. Every day. Not everything we want will fall from Heaven—far from it! And our daily bread won't fall directly into our open mouths. We must rise each morning and go out and gather for the day. We must work. We must cooperate with the One who feeds us. Jesus describes Himself in many ways, but one is the "Bread come down from Heaven"—the perfect fulfillment of what manna foreshadowed. In the Eucharist, He feeds us with His True Body and His True Blood so that we can have not just a home but a share in His divine life—everlasting life.

He'll lead you through the night

For just a little over forty years I lived in the Southern California desert. (Ironic, huh?) I know how expansive it can be, how dry and blazing hot, and how freezing at night in the winter. There are some scary creatures that come out of caves at night (and the local singles bars). When there's no moon, the night sky is as black as pitch. So that the Israelites would never lose their way, God led them through the desert darkness as a pillar of glowing fire at night and as a cloud in the sky by day. He will lead you too, if you open your eyes to Him.

You're going to have to go through a big change, if you have not already. You'll be smart to pack lightly and trust God to lead you. It will not be easy, but it will be worth the trek. A land flowing with milk and honey is waiting for *you*!

You can *change the way you think about God*

If you dive into the details of rebuilding a life without first seeing the big-picture truths, you greatly increase your chances of another divorce or at least a life of restless "wandering in the desert." The biggest reality is that you are here on this earth for God, and He is here for you. You can trust Him—even if you don't feel like it.

> I think I have learned to trust God more now than I did before. By trust I mean I don't panic or get as upset as I used to over things that go wrong because I am more inclined to see whatever happened as part of God's plan. I think I have a more open mind to opportunities that present themselves, both good and bad.
>
> —*J.C.*

> I think I'm learning to put more faith in God, to follow more hunches and opportunities as they come up. I'm seriously involved in overseas humanitarian mission work now, and I see myself using my writing and interpreting skills more and more to do God's work rather than client work. He's leading me down this

path and opening my heart wider than it's ever been opened before. This is one of several positive things that have happened in my life since the divorce.

—*Jeff*

The biggest thing I have learned through all of this is just to trust Him. It may not be my "plan." However, as they say, sometimes the best prayers are those that go unanswered. I put all of my trust in Our Lord.

—*P.R.*

I *know* that God has seen me through all of this, and I am so incredibly grateful. Some pretty amazing things happened, and I know they all came from God looking after me.

—*Patricia*

I'll let Jeff close this chapter with his advice:

The best single quote I came across in all of my reading during my post-divorce period was this: "Every crisis has a beginning, a middle and an end." I can't remember who wrote it. But it's a thought I took to heart. It makes a lot of sense. Even the worst days of your life eventually pass. They don't last forever.

Amen, Jeff.

Chapter 5

Let Your Father Be Your Architect

"Bye, Mom!" I hollered as I grabbed my plaid lunch pail and navy-blue uniform sweater and slammed the front door.

I was in third grade and walked to school every morning down El Camino Avenue to the stoplight, where I'd cross carefully and head five more blocks to the playground. About half way there I opened my lunch box and took out a shiny green apple. My favorite! CHOMP!

As I was chewing, I bit down onto something hard and unfamiliar, so I spat it out into my hand. With horror, I realized it was a dental filling, and my tongue probed around until it found a huge hole in one of my molars. It scared me. *Oh no*, I thought, *what now?* I knew I'd have to go to our family dentist, Dr. Worsely. I hated his office, where the room temperature was barely above freezing and the air held the faint scent of burning teeth and oral antiseptic. The last time I'd been in his chair and had heard the high-pitched whine of the metal drill, I'd cowered and squirmed and protested so much that he slapped me to make me sit still. I don't remember anything after that except that I *never* wanted to go back there again. Ever!

Now I was stuck at the street intersection, not knowing whether to cross or not. Mom wasn't home; she'd left right after I had to go downtown on errands. Dad was at work in his architectural and development firm, so our house was empty. Should I keep going on to school? What would Sister even know about my huge trauma? Did nuns have fillings? Would everyone make fun of me? I couldn't move forward or go back. I froze, holding back tears.

Part of me said, *Rosie, you have to find someone to help you!* Back in those days it was relatively safe to approach a stranger and ask for help. So I looked ahead at the cars that were stopped at the traffic light. It was a warm spring morning, and the car right in front had its windows rolled down. *I could call out to the driver, and he would hear me*, I thought, but before I could say "Excuse me, mister," I realized that car was my Dad's and the man sitting in the driver's seat was my father!

"Daddy!" I screamed, running to the side of the car and bursting into tears.

My father was surprised to see me, but he pulled slowly over to the curb, got out, and scooped me up in his arms. I buried my head in his chest and heaved uncontrollably. All he could hear were muffled sounds of "wah-h-h . . . filling . . . apple . . . don't make me go there . . . wah-h-h-h."

When I finally calmed down, Dad told me everything would be alright, and somehow I knew it would. In my father's arms the truth about having to see the dentist again became a manageable problem instead of the end of the world. Daddy always made everything okay, and I didn't have to worry anymore.

God can be trusted to help you rebuild

This might sound like a childish story that has nothing to do with adults trying to rebuild after a divorce. But at the heart of this true story is a central truth to your rebuilding: *God is a loving Father who can be trusted.* He *will* help you redesign and rebuild your life.

> God is a loving Father who can be trusted. He will help you redesign and rebuild your life.

Even in the constructing of a new life after a failed marriage, you will be tempted to focus primarily on what you can do to make a living, how much money you'll be able to make or keep, where and how the kids will get their needs met, or perhaps how you can make sure you have love again in your life. You will struggle with the temptation everyone faces: what can I do to be happy again? Should I go back? How can I go forward? Like me, you may be stuck at this current intersection and not be sure of which direction to take. The answer is always to look to the Father.

God designed the universe

No one can build a new house—or a new life—all alone. Smart people hire the best architect available, give him or her their vision and a list of necessities, and then work together to make the dream house come true. I know because my father was an architect and a builder, and *God the Father is your ultimate Architect when it comes to rebuilding something new after divorce.* His qualifications are stupendous: He not only drew up plans but then He created the universe—from nothing! He also knows you better than you know yourself. The trouble is that most people, like Adam and Eve, forget to trust God.

I want to take you back to the Old Testament again, to the story of Job. The Hebrews told rich and poetic tales to teach wisdom, and the story of Job involves a contest of sorts between God and the devil—with Job in the middle. (After going through a divorce, doesn't it seem like *you* are in the middle of a tug-of-war between good and evil?) Again, I hope you will read the book of

Job in the Bible for yourself, but since it's very long, I'll paraphrase it for you.

You probably recall that Job was a good man who loved the Lord. Job had a loving wife, ten children, many faithful servants, and huge herds of donkeys, camels, sheep, and oxen. He was rich, but it was God who was the primary focus of his life, not his family and great wealth. Scripture tells us that Job was honest and faithful and shunned evil.

One day God spoke with Satan, who had been prowling about the earth looking to distract and devour souls. God decided to brag a bit about Job's faithfulness, but Satan answered, "Well, of course he's faithful. You bless everything he does. You've given him everything he could ever want. Take it all way, however, and I bet he'll curse you."

God took Satan up on the bet, cautioning the devil to go ahead and strip Job of everything he owned but not to bring him any bodily harm. I like to imagine Satan howled with laughter, rubbed his hands together in wicked glee, and ran off to do his devastating work.

Shortly thereafter several messengers knocked on Job's door, bearing bad news:

"Some bandits stole most of the herds and killed the servants!"

"A huge fire burned the sheep and all the shepherds tending your flocks!"

"A freak wind storm brought the house down on

all your children and killed them as they were eating together! They're all dead."

Job was stunned! He'd lost his beautiful children and all his wealth. But then he quickly processed, grieved, and came to the conclusion that he'd come into this world with nothing and he would go out the same way. Knowing that God would somehow make all things right, Job fell to the ground in adoration and praise and blessed the name of God.

What faith! What trust! How many of us fell on our faces and blessed God after the losses of our divorce? I know I sure didn't. I always seemed to fall into the same cycle of panic, rage, and then tears of self-pity. But I'm learning.

But Job's testing didn't end there. Satan persisted, and the next time Job was struck from the top of his head to the bottom of his feet with oozing, painful ulcers. He sat in a pile of ashes and used the rough edge of a clay pot to scrape off the scabs. He was utterly miserable. His wife—not being as faithful as Job—nagged at him, "Oh, stop being so holy. Look at you! Look what God is permitting to happen to you while you go on praising Him. Just curse Him and get it over with!" Perhaps in his heart Job was beginning to wonder.

For the next seven days and nights, his neighbors, who could hardly recognize their old friend, sat quietly with him in his misery. Job finally fell into a deep melancholy and broke the silence with a curse—not of God but of the day he'd been born. He wailed and wept as he decried his birth, wishing he'd been stillborn. "Why couldn't I have been born dead, a child put away from my mother's womb so I'd never have to see the misery of this life?"

His friends tried to comfort him, but Job persisted in questioning why this had all happened to him. Finally Job decided that somehow God had wronged him and that he *deserved* better.

At this, God appeared. I imagine they *all* fell to their faces, shivering and shaking like Dorothy and her companions in front of the great and powerful Wizard of Oz. I think God could still "look" Job straight in the face, locking eyes, even as Job lay prostrate. His voice must have been terrifying and exhilarating at the same time. The time for Job to demand answers from God was over. The Master Architect was about to show how He didn't just do good and marvelous things in the world—He DESIGNED and BUILT everything in the universe!

The following words are God's. Please take your time reading each line; they are beautiful and powerful reminders that God is God and He *can* be trusted:

Who is this that darkens counsel by words without knowledge?

Gird up your loins like a man, I will question you, and you shall declare to me. "Where were you when I laid the foundation of the earth? Tell me, *if you have understanding*.

Who determined its measurements—surely you know! Or who stretched the line upon it? On what were its bases sunk, or who laid its cornerstone, when the morning stars sang together, and all the sons of God shouted for joy?

Or who shut in the sea with doors, when it burst forth from the womb; when I made clouds its garment, and thick darkness its swaddling band, and prescribed bounds for it, and set bars and doors, and said, Thus far shall you come, and no farther, and here shall your proud waves be stayed?

Have you commanded the morning since your days began, and caused the dawn to know its place, that it might take hold of the skirts of the earth, and the wicked be shaken out of it?. . .

Have you comprehended the expanse of the earth? Declare, if you know all this. . . .

And the LORD said to Job: "Shall a faultfinder contend with the Almighty? He who argues with God, let him answer it."

Father really does know best

Poor Job! My mom used to sit us down and give us long lectures, but they were nothing like the one God gave Job. Job needed to be set straight in his think-ing about who he was before God. Not because God wanted to "lord it over him" but to steer him away from the self-centered thinking that leads to life apart from God—spiritual death. God barked and scowled and let Job shiver in his boots *out of love.*

My warm, loving father had a tough side, too. From his career as an architect and land developer, Dad set-tled into a commercial real estate appraisal business, where I ended up working with him for over twenty years. During the first few years I noticed that one of the men who worked with us was not pulling his weight the way I thought he should, and he even appeared to be falsifying job records. So I took it upon myself to tell Dad what we needed to do with the man. At first Dad seemed irritated with my advice, but I pressed in, ratio-nalizing that I had every right to approach Dad about running the business. After all, I wanted the company to thrive, I was his daughter, and I was certainly pull-ing *my* weight—and then some. This went on for a few months, with me continuing to complain to my father. I actually questioned why he was allowing this man to continue to even work with us. One day, instead of his usual tolerant listening, Dad barked back.

"Listen, Rosie! *You don't know everything!*"

Whoa! My eyes widened, and I shut up.

"Where were you when I started this business? Where were you when I built it up? Whose name is on the front door? This is my business, and I'll run it any way I want!"

I protested, but my voice was cracking and becoming high-pitched. "Dad! He's *bad news* for our company! *You know that*!" Why was Dad being so mean to me?

Dad stared at me with the sternest look I think I'd ever seen.

"If you don't like it, then you can leave. In fact . . . YOU'RE FIRED."

What? I was in shock, hurt, and angry.

"FINE!" I ran to my desk, grabbed my purse and car keys, and drove home in the middle of the day. When I got home I threw myself on the bed and sobbed and sobbed. After dinner I ate three bowls of coffee ice cream and went to bed early.

The next morning I got up, washed my face, and stared into the mirror. It was that moment of reality that many people avoid. It was a fresh, new day and I took inventory:

◇ Dad loves me. I love him.
◇ I'm right about the guy, but Dad's right about the business being his.
◇ My Dad has never let me down. I need to trust him.
◇ I should be thankful I even work there!
◇ He's given me a career for life if I want.
◇ Maybe Dad has some way of dealing with the guy I don't know.

◇ Would it kill me if the man still worked there?

I took a shower, got dressed, drove to the office, and walked in. I put my purse on my desk and got a cup of coffee. Then I went up to Dad, who was sitting at his big mahogany desk, looked him right in the eyes, and said, "Dad . . . I'm sorry. I love you."

My father swiveled around in his chair to face me, gave me a tender look, and said, "No, honey, *I'm* sorry. And I love you too. Sometimes I'm just a grumpy old man."

"No, Dad, sometimes I'm a pushy oldest daughter!"

Even though I was in my twenties, I crawled onto his lap and we laughed and hugged.

"Now sit down a minute," he said. "I want to tell you something."

I moved over to a chair near his desk and listened. I was uncharacteristically humble and quiet.

"This man has problems. I didn't want to tell you because—quite frankly—it's none of your business." Dad punctuated with a direct look. I grinned sheepishly.

"He's got a history of drug and alcohol abuse and has been trying to get sober. He has two little girls, and his wife left him. I feel badly for him and want to help. I know he's been lying about some things and has not been doing the best job. I see what you see. But I've been talking with him privately and I'm not about to give up on him yet. I won't let this company be seriously jeopardized and—if I have to—I *will* fire him. But not yet."

"Oh, Dad, I'm sorry. I didn't know."

"I know, honey, but you have to trust me. I've been around a lot longer than you have."

"I know."

"And I appreciate all you do here for this company, and I'm proud of you in so many ways."

"Thanks, Dad."

I'd thought I was so smart. I also thought I knew my father, but there was so much I did not know. As I became more of an adult and worked side by side with him for the next few decades, Dad revealed more of himself to me. God does the same thing with us.

Just as I didn't know the innermost thoughts of my Dad, we often don't know God very well, either. We don't want a scary God who reminds us how selfishly we are seeing things or how big we are getting for our own britches. We want a warm fuzzy Father—a benevolent, ever-tolerant God. But the reality is that God is both—for our own good. And always out of sheer love for us, His children.

Job answers God

Poor Job. Just as he was getting ready to tell God what he thought, God lowered the boom, as my own father did to me. But Job's heart was open, and he once again realized that God was smarter, more powerful, and could always be trusted. Job admitted he didn't really know God and humbly responded to Him in thanksgiving. When he did, God restored all that he'd lost—and then doubled it!

The end of Job's story should give you hope. When we return to God in humility, He embraces us and blesses us with more gifts than ever. Does that mean you'll get the house, money, car, kids, and other losses back after your divorce? Maybe, maybe not. But remember that the things of this world pale in comparison to the eternal gifts God has for us.

You might not get the house back, but you'll have a warm, safe place to live.

You might not get the money back, but your basic needs will be met.

You might not get a new spouse, but you will always have *someone* to love.

Your heavenly Father knows what is good for you, and He will give you double and triple portions of these things: love, mercy, grace, virtues, wisdom, and much more.

Chapter 6

Enjoy Making Plans

SHOULD God make all our decisions for us? On one level Scripture does advise us to be skeptical about our own judgment. Proverbs 3:5–7 declares, "Trust in the LORD with all your heart, and do not rely on your own insight. In all your ways acknowledge him, and he will make straight your paths. Be not wise in your own eyes; fear the LORD, and turn away from evil."

Yet in many other places—like Proverbs 3:13–14— we're told to seek wisdom and exercise good judgment. "Happy is the man who finds wisdom, and the man who gets understanding, for the gain from it is better than gain from silver and its profit better than gold."

When life is tough, it may seem easier to ask God to make all of our decisions for us. But then we'd become wooden puppets and never know the joys of true freedom, which is the ability to choose what is good, true, and beautiful. Although we must build our foundation on God and live within the guidelines He gives us through the Church, our lives don't have to be like a boring tract house. God's gift of our free will allows us to "pick our own floor plan" when we rebuild our lives after a divorce. We get to make personal choices about where we live, what we do for work and fun, and who we will choose for friends. If you've ever bought a new home, you know

> When life is tough, it may seem easier to ask God to make all of our decisions for us

the builder has already determined some general sizes and layouts and what basic materials will be used, but he knows this is where *you* will live and wants you to make it yours. You get to pick the floor plan, the paint color, the tile, the carpet, and so much more.

However, some people are afraid to make even small decisions after divorce, and they put the final say back in God's lap. They may feel they have made some bad mistakes in the past—and perhaps they have—but God still wants us to use our heads and make sound judgments. Sure, there are times we must step in—out of love—to decide for someone. But planning and choosing every detail of someone's life can often be unloving: it can keep them from growing mentally, emotionally, or spiritually.

Does God really have a plan for you?

I frequently hear divorced men and women lament about God's plans having gone awry, "God brought us together. Why, then, did He allow this divorce?"

Patricia, like so many, shared with me in one of my divorce groups: "I know God has a plan in all this. But I wish I knew what it was!"

Some who have been severely abused in their marriage and are relieved to be divorced will often cite, "God must have always had some better plan for me!"

When people are in pain, they turn to God, and that's good. Wanting to know His will for us is good. But God's will is not necessarily a specific person, place, or plan. Desiring such specifics can be a way of avoiding personal responsibility, like those who want everything so clearly spelled out that they don't have to think for themselves. "Just tell me, God, what do you want? Show me a sign. Tell me your plan. I won't move until you do." Staying put and waiting for God may be the wise thing to do. But sometimes we become paralyzed and refuse to move without God doing all the work for us. No risk of skinned shins for us! We want Him holding the back of our bikes forever.

God has already told us what He wants for us: Heaven, that loving, intimate union with Him now and forever. He's told us in general terms how to get there, but because we are all unique and unrepeatable per-

sons—with different longings, talents, and treasures—
we can have a variety of choices that are all in keeping
with His will for us. It's God's fatherhood that shows
us that.

God is a Father, not a puppet master

If you can't tell by now, my father, Rowland, seemed
bigger than life to me and my eight brothers and sisters.
We loved Dad, and from the time we were young we
longed to be close to him, often fighting to be the one
to sit on his lap. Over the years we each spent intimate
time with him in different ways.

Dad loved to play golf so my brother John spent
hours with him hitting buckets of balls on the driving
range. Dad was delighted to spend time with his son
there. But our father didn't insist that the rest of us take
up golf and be just like John.

Another brother, Charlie, loved to fly airplanes, and
some of the best times Charlie had with Dad were in
the air.

I have a fear of heights and can't hit a golf ball worth
beans, so thankfully Dad never said, "Rosie, what's
wrong with you? Why can't you be with me like your
brothers?" Instead, I got to choose the specific way I
lived out my relationship with Dad—in the family real
estate business, working together on projects and solving
problems, going out for expensive dinners every once in

a while, and laughing together at my father's jokes.

When each of us began to choose our life careers, Dad would never tell us what to do unless he saw us in danger of making a grave moral mistake. Then he'd tell us as bluntly as possible that we were being—well, I can't repeat what he said, but let's just say—stupid.

Dad also didn't try to arrange our marriages. It gave him pleasure to have us freely choose whom we would love and marry. When we came to him with our intended spouse, sometimes he'd warn us that he thought the person we had fallen in love with was not grown up enough—or too selfish—to be married. Sadly, most of us didn't listen, but Dad refused to interfere with our free choice. In other less important matters he would simply tell us to search our hearts and use our heads. No matter our choices, Dad always loved us and would stand by us, permitting us to suffer the natural consequences of our choices. If necessary, he'd call us back to a higher level and help us get back on track. Again and again, if that's what it took.

The way we respond to our Father God—our intimate union with Him—will look and play out differently for each of us who are His children. And as long as we search our hearts (for sinful selfishness) and use the brains God gave us (assuming they are properly and well-informed), our life choices can include a wide range of selections that are all pleasing to Him. Sometimes there are many different career paths, people to marry, and places to live that are in conformance with His will for us.

God's will—His plan for us—is that we learn to love as He loves. There are many good ways we can do that, and it delights Him to let us choose what we like. God gives us our life as an "allowance," and He gives us the freedom to spend it as we wish.

Remember Adam and Eve? God gave them a whole garden full of trees that had a wide variety of delicious fruit from which they could eat. They did not wake up each morning and pray, "Oh, Lord, tell us from which tree to eat today. We want to know your will. Give us a sign." He already outlined what was good and not good and gave them permission to eat *as they wished*—all from one tree if they wanted or from several at a time. On Tuesday they could eat red fruit, on Wednesday just the yellow. It didn't really matter. They could freely choose to their own delight, and that gave Him pleasure. It was only the one tree—the tree of the knowledge of good and evil—that He forbade. And He made His plan very clear. They didn't need a sign to know His will.

God's perfect will and His permissive will

My father hoped we would all go to college and achieve great and noble careers. He knew the blessings that could come to us that way and the good we could do in the world. You might say that was his "perfect will" for his children. But only Fred, the youngest, went to medical school, and he became one of the top spine surgeons in the country. Dad's "permissive will" was that we could choose our own path. The rest of us ended up in a variety of not-very-glamorous careers, but we each chose a field where we could give of ourselves to others and be a blessing to others. Dad instilled that in each of us by his counsel and personal example. And before my father died in 2003, he was pleased with his children, despite our failures and imperfections. In a letter he wrote me he said, "I have always prayed that my sons and daughters would be servants and handmaidens of the Lord. I'm happy to say that I can be proud of all of you in that regard."

Dad had lofty and perfect goals for us, but he didn't force us. He permitted us to choose where we would go in life, as long as it was something that would not prevent or obstruct moving our minds and hearts closer to God. The Church teaches that our Father God also has a perfect will—that which would be the best good in a situation—and a permissive will—one that allows us to choose. If we choose some form of authentic good, great! If we unfortunately choose evil (putting our self first over Him and everyone), God still promises to be there to bring greater good out of the sinful failures of those who love Him and seek His forgiveness. Does that mean we get to sin and not worry about anything? No. You know that.

God speaks His will, His plan for us, in many ways: through His words to us preserved in Sacred Scripture and Tradition, through the teachings of our Mother, the Church, and through wise and holy teachers who may be our parents, counselors, friends, and family. If we pray sincerely to want to know God and His plan for us, He will answer. If we listen to God's voice and heed His wisdom long enough, some of that wisdom supernaturally infuses itself into our hearts so that tough decision-making becomes easier and easier—and always according to His plan.

Dear God, send me a soul mate

After divorce, many want to know if God has a plan to bring them someone new to love. In my book for singles, *Dear God, Send Me a Soul Mate*,[1] I advised the reader that there is no such thing as one perfect person who God predestined for us. Indeed, there may be many who would make a suitable spouse for us, given maturity, ability, and God's grace working in their hearts. After a divorce, some may have more than a small fear that God originally had only one person in the universe who was to be their spouse—that God brought them together and now they blew it (or their spouse did) and they will never find happiness again. How depressing if that were the truth! But with right intention, maturity, and ability, there can be a number of potential spouses whom you could love and with whom you could have a good and holy marriage.

The person you marry is the right one—and God's choice in that He gave *you* the freedom to choose—assuming you both enter marriage rightly as the Church prescribes. Even when you find out there is something not quite "right" about someone you married, grace empowers you to love him or her anyway.

Some people marry for wrong and selfish reasons or permanently hold back part of themselves from their spouse. Some simply don't have the ability to enter into and live out marriage as the Church defines it. In such cases, the Church can investigate and declare (through the annulment process) that no true marriage bond was created when you both said "I do."

Your prior marriage may be valid, despite the separation or divorce, but in your opinion, it may have been wrong and you're ready for love again. That's where we need to be careful because we *don't* always know the whole truth. In the eyes of the Church you may still be married and forbidden to pursue romance with another. Ever. These are harsh words that no one wants to hear. This can be an excruciatingly difficult cross to bear but one that is not impossible with grace and one that can bear much fruit in your life. We cover more about this in chapter 11. If you haven't done so, please go talk to your pastor or another wise and holy priest who can give you good spiritual direction. If you try to rebuild without discerning your situation, your future life could be filled with nagging doubt, growing fear, anxiety, guilt, shame, anger, and self-deception that you might want to cover up with eating, drinking, spending, or other self-medication. Whew!

Anxiety about finding someone new will enslave you. Even though it might not feel like it, it can push you into a relationship that seems delicious at first but will bring its own form of rot to the souls involved. It might help to know you were not ultimately made for earthly marriage; you were made for an eternal, mystical "marriage" to God—an intimate union of your mind and heart with Him. Earthly marriage can be a blessing and joy, but it will give way in the end to something greater and sweeter: an everlasting communion with God and the saints in Heaven. In marriage on the earth, we get to taste only a little bit of Heaven. Don't be anxious about enjoying the hors d'oeuvres; God has prepared a banquet for you.

Please remember that God knew ahead of time who you would choose in this life and what would happen to you. But He doesn't act as the grand puppet master in the sky, bringing together by perfect circumstances people who are predestined to marry. He's also not the clutching "smother mother" who controls exactly what video game her child will buy with his or her allowance. Instead He gives us general guidelines and a wide berth, permitting us to choose whom we love and marry. He promises to bless the union if we enter it rightly. He also promises to let us carry the cross of our own sinful choices or careless mistakes, learn from them, and bring greater good out of any mess we make. He calls us back—again and again—to a higher level of learning to love as He loves. He truly is our Father.

Chapter 7

Lay a Firm Foundation

I'LL never forget watching the house in which I'd been born being slowly carried down the street on a long truck bed. I was just five years old, and Daddy had donated our small home to the Institute of the Blessed Virgin Mary sisters who'd come to our diocese from Chicago. They were going to establish Our Lady of the Assumption elementary school, where I would eventually attend, and they needed a convent. My parents gave them one.

A week before the move, workers had rushed to pour the concrete and ready the site for the new house. I sat with my mother in the front seat of our 1953 Oldsmobile from across the street and watched the movers lower the house down on the new foundation that was ready to receive the structure. BOOM! When the dust settled, the house looked like it had been there for years.

What is your foundation?

No house can stand without a firm foundation. No life can survive divorce—and all the trials of this world—without a foundation in Christ. But our fallen nature, inherited from Adam and Eve, is to lack trust in God and to decide for ourselves what is good or not good.

"Often man does not build his actions and his existence on Jesus, but prefers the sands of ideology, power, success, and money." This was a warning in a March 2011 talk by the Holy Father Pope Benedict XVI that temporal goods can never serve as a solid foundation for life. These things are truly sand—not solid rock—and they will never hold up under great stress. But even "good Catholics" can place far too much weight on relationships, career, heath, sex, and pleasure (and you know the rest) to be the basis of our security and happiness.

> Jesus came to tell us that if we would build on *Him*, we'd be safe and joyful.

I certainly made the kids the center of my life after the divorce. But I think my volunteer work is bringing more balance to the equation. I'm also much more likely to let my kids go to friends' houses for sleepovers, etc. than I was a couple of years ago. They are getting older, and I am making an effort to give them more space.

—Jeff

Due to some bad influences I put myself in harm's way by believing the lie that casual sex brings you the things you desire. Now, in retrospect, all I can say is UGH! So I would say I made sexual promiscuity a false idol, a false foundation for happiness.

—Anonymous

But Jesus came to tell us that if we would build on *Him*, we'd be safe and joyful.

Every one who comes to me and hears my words and does them, I will show you what he is like: he is like a man building a house, who dug deep, and laid the foundation upon rock; and when a flood arose, the stream broke against that house, and could not shake it, because it had been well built. But he who hears and does not do them is like a man who built a house on the ground without a foundation; against which the stream broke, and immediately it fell, and the ruin of that house was great.

—Luke 6:47–49

When divorce exposes false foundations, we can learn not to try to rebuild on them again. That's what I did when I had my adult conversion experience. Finally tired of the cracks that kept appearing in my life, I let God lift me up off of the old, crumbling concrete of my own ego and all the cultural icons on which I'd built my life. He lifts us up and lays us down where we should have been in the first place: resting securely on the cornerstone of His Son, Jesus.

Jesus the cornerstone

"The stone which the builders rejected has become the head of the corner."

—Psalm 118:22

The cornerstone (or foundation stone) is the first stone set in the construction of a masonry foundation. It's the most vital since all other stones will be set in reference to this stone; thus it determines the design and stability of the entire structure. Walls, roof, and interior improvements can't be erected without this solid bedrock. If your foundation is not centered in Christ, your life will most certainly crack, crumble, or come crashing down when the earthquakes or floods hit. The problem is that many of us know about Christ but do not know Him personally.

Jesus can remain a biblical figure who seems rather dull and boring, someone who was around a long, long time ago. But that is the lie that keeps us uninterested in the One with whom we were meant to have the most adventurous and passionate relationship ever. We were made to burn hotly with love for Christ, to open up to receive Him, and to give ourselves in wild abandon to His love. To sell all we own and follow Him into battle, and to lay down our lives on the battlefield with Him. Instead, we yawn.

None of us will ever make Jesus the center of our lives unless we first know Him, begin to love Him, and see that we can trust Him. How do *you* feel about Jesus, really? What do you know about Him?

Knowing Jesus for the first time

I was seven when I recall being excited about Jesus.

"When you receive the Host, you will be receiving Jesus in a very special way. He wants to come into your heart and live there forever," said Sister, smiling angelically.

I was sitting with thirty-five other uniform-clad second-graders and was being prepared for my first Holy Communion at Our Lady of the Assumption school in Carmichael, California. Sister's face, framed by the starched, black-and-white habit, glowed when she spoke of Jesus. I imagined that hidden below her hemline, her feet were probably hovering just above the floor. I looked around the classroom at the beautiful biblical scenes of Jesus curing crippled children, walking on water, and hanging on the Cross. His Sacred Heart was on fire. Sister was on fire. I wanted to be on fire too. It was a mystical moment for me, and I made a decision to ask Jesus into my heart so He could live there forever.

But forever didn't last very long. I was a typical Catholic school girl who said my prayers until I reached puberty. It was the turbulent sixties, and I was constantly assaulted by the culture to rebel against authority, reject Rome, burn my bra, and do whatever felt good. Just as there are today, there were so many distractions and delicious temptations that were seducing me away from my faith. The times angrily elevated women's rights, ignored women's responsibilities, and ridiculed what was called patriarchal religion. I didn't understand it all and, frankly, wasn't that interested in politics and religion. Not when you could pursue the pleasures of making money and spending it at the mall. Prayers gave way to parties; God gave way to self. Sure, Jesus was still in my heart, but I had relegated him to the cellar, where I would call on Him only in case of emergency.

Have you ever gone through a period like that in your life? Has your faith been part-time or weak? Maybe you've been a regular church-goer but the focus has been on religious activity rather than a deeply intimate relationship with God. Like me, maybe your divorce has shaken you up enough that you've run right down into the cellar of your life and hollered, "Okay, Jesus, you can come out now. I need you!"

Or maybe worse, Jesus has become Hugo the rat man, whom you hire just for a short time to come clean up the nest of rodents—the ex, the courts, the bank— that are stinking up the crawl space in your life. When things calm down or you win in court or get a new relationship, Hugo can go back to the office until you need him again. Something is very wrong with this way of thinking.

Jesus is not a vending machine

In this way of thinking, the center of the universe is not God. It's me. And it's not about what He wants for us, but *what we want*. Often we only look to God to get us what we think we need. Heaven is too far away, and we can't wait that long. We're hungry or lonely or tired. We want it here and now. Especially after divorce, when we feel most emptied.

Sadly, God can become reduced to a divine vending machine to get us what we want. We send up prayers, rosaries, and novenas like they were nickels, dimes, and dollars and ask that God send us what we want. But God is not a vending machine. He is not another thing we have in our life with all the other things. He's not the thing we do on Sunday. He's revealed Himself to us in many ways. How can you get to really know Him? The same way you get to know and trust anyone:

◇ Start to spend time alone with Him
◇ Talk to Him
◇ Ask Him questions
◇ Listen to what He says about Himself and you
◇ See how He handles Himself with others
◇ Pay attention to how He relates to you
◇ Read what others have written about Him
◇ Interview His friends
◇ Inspect His work
◇ Call His Mother!

All the information you need to know about Him has been carefully and faithfully preserved and passed on by Holy Mother, the Church. Under the guidance of the Holy Spirit, the Church has given us the Bible, which tells us how utterly wonderful He is. Read just a few of the following descriptions, and you won't be able to help yourself. You may not fully trust it, but you must agree—He sounds perfect. (And He is!)

Advocate – *He fights evil for us on our behalf.*
1 John 2:1
Almighty – *He is Most Powerful, Most High.*
Apocalypse 1:8

Alpha and Omega – *He is our beginning and our end. We came from Him, we are going to Him.* Apocalypse 1:8

Author and Perfecter of our Faith – *He never gives up on helping us know Him.* Hebrews 12:2

Bread of Life – *He satisfies the hungry heart.* John 6:35, 48

Bridegroom – *He loves us with a passionate love and wants us to "be His" forever.* Matthew 9:15

Comforter – *He dries our tears and gives us hope.* Jeremiah 8:18

Cornerstone – *Everything centers on Him.* Ephesians 2:20

Deliverer – *He went to His death to save us from slavery and death.* Romans 11:26

Emmanuel – *He is God come to be "with us," always and everywhere.* Matthew 1:23

Everlasting Father – *He gives us life and protects, guides, and delights in us.* Isaiah 9:6

Fountain – *All life and love flows abundantly from Him.* Zechariah 13:1

Friend of Sinners – *He approaches us even when we fail Him.* Matthew 11:19

God – *There is not and never will be any like Him.* John 1:1

Good Shepherd – *He guides us to true food*

and true shelter. John 10:11

High Priest – *He stands before God to make the sacrifice we could not.* Hebrews 3:1

Holy One of Israel – *He is utterly and mysteriously Holy, Holy, Holy!* Isaiah 41:14

King of Kings – *All authority and all loving leadership flows from Him.* 1 Timothy 6:15; Apocalypse 19:16

Lamb of God – *He allowed Himself to be slain and sacrificed to save us.* John 1:29

Last Adam – *By His obedience to the Father, He undid what the first Adam did.* 1 Corinthians 15:45

Life – *He is life itself.* John 11:25

Light of the World – *He brings us out of all darkness.* John 8:12; John 9:5

Lion of the Tribe of Judah – *He is fierce and powerful and ready to devour evil to save us.* Apocalypse 5:5

Lord of Lords – *He is the ultimate in generous providence.* 1 Timothy 6:15; Apocalypse 19:16

Master – *He is the ultimate caretaker of souls—we owe Him all.* Matthew 23:8

Messiah – *He solves all problems, conquers all evil.* John 1:41

Morning Star – *He is the beauty of all that is bright and beautiful.* Apocalypse 22:16

Physician – *He can, and wants to, heal any broken heart.* Matthew 9:12

Prince of Peace – *He calms the storm that rages in our minds and hearts.* Isaiah 9:6

Purifier – *He wants to make us pure and perfect and free us from all evil.* Malachi 3:3

Rabbi – *He loves to draw close and teach us.* John 1:49

Redeemer – *He paid the price in full to redeem us from our evil captor.* Isaiah 41:14

Refiner – *His love is like a fire that burns.* Malachi 3:2

Refuge – *He is where we can safely hide when we are pursued by evil.* Isaiah 25:4

Resurrection – *He is the promise of our new life.* John 11:25

Righteousness – *He is total Good.* Jeremiah 23:6

Rock – *He is solid and never changing. He gives us perfect security.* Deuteronomy 32:4

Seed of the Woman – *He is the promise to Adam and Eve and us all.* Genesis 3:15

Servant – *He is true humility, ready to offer Himself as a gift.* Isaiah 42:1

Son of God – *He has an intimate and loving union with God the Father.* Luke 1:35

Son of Mary – *He is like us in every way,*

except sin. Mark 6:3

Truth – *He is the unchanging, reliable fact.* John 14:6

Way – *He is how we get to Heaven.* John 14:6

Wonderful Counselor – *He is amazing in how He enlightens us.* Isaiah 9:6

Word – *He is all meaning, all communication, that comes from God.* John 1:1

Vine – *He is both root and branches, and we are branches "in Him."* John 15:1

He is the One we all want, whether we realize it or not. If you think you want a fiery new life filled with adventure and passion, purpose that has deep meaning and satisfaction, love that rises to the highest heights, and peace that surpasses all understanding, then realize those are just some of the fruits of a relationship with Him. It's really not these *things* you want, you really want Him.

And He wants you.

Chapter 8

Work from God's Blueprints

"Dad, may I please borrow a thousand dollars?" That's the question I asked my father after my first divorce. I wanted to move into an apartment and needed to cover first and last months' rent and other moving expenses.

He was quick to answer. "No, honey, but if you work for me for a month, I'll pay you the thousand dollars. You can type, can't you?"

No, I *couldn't* type and that's not the answer I wanted to hear—but I needed the money. It was the 1970s and my father would smoke his big, fat cigar while rough-ing-out his commercial real estate appraisal reports with his big, fat fingers on an old Olivetti typewriter. Click-ety-click-click. There were no personal computers back then, so Dad had paid a professional secretary a thou-sand dollars a month to type finish quality reports for the client. I reluctantly agreed to take the job and spent a month typing the best I could. I soon became fasci-nated by the local lore and interesting facts about real estate in the Southern California desert where we lived. I also typed the invoices he sent to clients, and I was shocked to see he billed an average fee of five thousand dollars per report. I decided I wanted to be an appraiser! He agreed, and one of the first things he taught me was how to read a set of construction blueprints.

"Architecture is about the creative design and concept; engineering is taking that design and integrating all of the different building systems, like the floors, walls and roof (structure), the mechanical improvements, or the electrical system."

Yada, yada, yada . . . I heard what Dad was saying, but it was that big roll of construction plans laid out on the worktable in front of us that interested me. We were appraising an office building, and I could tell from the pictures on the blueprints where the building sat on the lot, where the parking lot was, and those little squiggly things? Palm trees. From the drawings I could measure the office building's square foot area that we needed for the assignment. It wasn't difficult; it just took some time, and I needed an expert to teach me how to decipher the engineer's hieroglyphics.

Before the invention of blueprints in the 1800s, which allowed copying of architectural plans, construction was an extremely slow process. There was only one set of drawings for all the contractors and workers. But with blueprints, everyone could have his own copy from which to work. Although there are even newer methods used today, blueprints made the job of building faster and easier, going hand-in-hand with the tremendous growth during the twentieth century.

I shared this part of my life with Dad because it's a perfect illustration of why we need blueprints for rebuilding our lives after divorce—and why we need someone to teach us how to read them.

It's the Church who gives us our blueprints for life

Some people are deeply wounded by those in their church after a divorce. They face ridicule, shame, rejection, and worse. Because of this, you might have to move to another parish or go to another priest for the Sacraments. Regardless, you must learn to forgive those who fail you and your family in that way. Those imperfect people are *in* the Church, but they themselves are not "The Church." The Church is the Bride of Christ, and she has been under attack from the start. She walks with a limp, but she is still loved and protected by her Spouse.

Though the Church is the Bride of Christ, and our Mother, we might also think of her as the "engineer" who has been given the task of taking the Master Architect's creative design for the human family and laying it out into the various systems that make up the warm and safe place for us to live. From God's design for us, and under the direction of the Holy Spirit, She has given us the blueprints for our lives.

But these blueprints are much more than a pre-scribed way to live so that we can be happy. They are the divine revelation of God's own heart to His people. The *Catechism of the Catholic Church* tells us that God reveals Himself out of love for us in two distinct modes: Sacred Scripture and Sacred Tradition.

Sacred Scripture: The written Word of God

"Sacred Scripture is the speech of God as it is put down in writing under the breath of the Holy Spirit."

—*CCC* 81

Scripture tells us of God's love and His plan for us to get back home to Heaven. The books of the Bible have been given to the world as blueprints for how we are to love one another in a way that will bring us true happiness. When the printing press was invented—much like the invention of blueprints—everyone could have a copy. But it's important to remember that the entire Bible foretells, or points to, and is about Jesus Himself. He is the single perfect Word spoken by God through all eternity. He *is* the living blueprint.

Sacred Tradition: The oral teachings of Jesus and His disciples

"[Sacred] Tradition transmits in its entirety the Word of God which has been entrusted to the apostles by Christ the Lord and the Holy Spirit."

—*CCC* 81

The Bible isn't everything we know about Christ. Imagine thinking that reading someone's diary is the only way to really learn about him. Diaries reveal a lot, but talking with that person's friends and family is just as important. The Gospel of John tells us that not everything Jesus said and did was written down, but much of it passed faithfully by word of mouth from His friends and family—the disciples and succeeding generations—right down to today.

But what if someone wants to build his or her life on what God has revealed and becomes confused? What if two or more cannot agree on what the blueprints mean? Aha! God already knew that could—and would—happen, and so Jesus put the Church in charge.

The Magisterium: The teaching authority of the Church

The task of giving an authentic interpretation of the Word of God, whether in its written form or in the form of Tradition, has been entrusted to the living, teaching office of the Church alone. Its authority in this matter is exercised in the name of Jesus Christ.

—*CCC* 85

Jesus promised that no one would ever take the Church down, even though She might stumble, She falls under the eternal protection of the Holy Spirit. Using our building analogy, the Holy Spirit might be likened to the inspector on a construction project. He knows the architectural design and the necessary engineering, and He makes sure no error is made in the really important parts of the structure. Imagine some carpenters who slacked off on the job, cut corners, or otherwise did a shoddy job. No worry, the building inspector will eventually come along and make things right. Likewise, although there can be leaders or others in the Church who make problems, the Building Inspector makes sure that the foundation, walls, and roof—the most important parts—are always built to code. The official teachings of the Church can never be in error. What a relief that is!

This three-pronged system of truth has helped me, as it can help you, rebuild a life that is rich and satisfying after a divorce. Not only that, your house will stand when the storms of life blow strong and hard again— and they will.

But sadly, some think the Church is too rigid.

◇ Oh, sacred this and sacred that, and how do you even spell *magisterium* anyway?
◇ Can't I just be a good person and have my own private relationship with God?
◇ There are too many systems, too many regulations. Get with the times!

◇ Who needs all those blueprints with all those endless little details?

◇ Why do I need an inspector to tell me how to live? That's between me and Jesus.

Please don't try to build a new life after your divorce on your own. Your new house will not stand the hurricanes, nor the rats or little termites that may come to rot it from the inside out. I tried that, and I ended up divorced again. Don't make the mistakes I've made. The Church is not here to control you but to protect you. It's Her job!

I was very successful as an appraiser, enjoyed a good professional reputation in the industry, and made a lot of money. I had a career that provided me with job satisfaction and financial security. But I never would have had that life had I not submitted—yes, that dreaded word SUBMIT—myself to a similar three-pronged system. Consider this:

Even though I was a smart, young apprentice appraiser, I still needed guidance in reading blueprints and interpreting real estate market trends, especially when I made mistakes.

◇ How prideful I would have been to try to figure things out myself and not take advantage of my father's many years of being a successful appraiser. *He was like the teaching Magisterium.*

⋄ How stupid to never read the history of appraisal techniques, open a cost manual, research market data, or subscribe to a monthly appraisal organization newsletter. *Those things are like Sacred Scripture.*

⋄ How arrogant I would have been not to regularly attend meetings with other appraisers and belong to appraisal industry groups. I can't tell you the things I learned—the inside scoop—from hearing about other appraisers' experiences. Their stories made me laugh, inspired me to be a better appraiser, and helped me to become a highly-paid expert witness in state and federal courts in real estate valuation. *They are like Sacred Tradition.*

If you find yourself resisting the Church's wisdom and guidance in matters of love, sexuality, marriage, divorce, annulments, sin, and confession—or any other area where you may be confused, angry, or shut down—ask God to help break down the barriers that may come from fear or pride.

Two thousand years and counting

Divorce problems are not new. We humans have been stumbling and falling since our beginning, and God continues to be there to pick us up. He made us,

He knows us, He came to us in person, and He left us His Church to guide us. With over two thousand years of wisdom and experience, and under the direct guidance of the Holy Spirit, She's still (and always will be) in the business of helping people rebuild. There *are* no better blueprints than those She has for us.

When I shared this rebuilding analogy with Judy, who is divorced, and asked if she'd ever built a home, she told me, "Yes, I have been involved in building a home, but I must admit I cannot make heads or tails out of reading blueprints!" Like my Dad helped me—and the Church has helped us all for centuries—I promise to help you read the blueprints and make both heads *and* tails of them!

Chapter 9

Expect an Adequate Timeframe

"DEVASTATION!" Yesterday that was the headline on the front page of the San Francisco Chronicle reporting the deadly 9.0 earthquake and subsequent tsunami that pounded Japan and terrorized the Pacific Rim from Asia to California. Large colored photos plastered all over television and the Internet showed the devastation that killed hundreds, flattened buildings, and left an overwhelming and muddy mess. Not only that, but the giant ocean waves pushed eastward past Hawaii and over five thousand miles to the California coast, destroying beachfront marinas, boats, and killing some who were trying to save their property.

Divorce is a similar devastation. There are the hard, direct hits and the long-reaching collateral damage to friends, family members, the children, and the community—and even into the next generations. In rebuilding your life, you'll want to keep your eyes open for areas that may have been directly hit by the divorce—like losing a spouse, your home, or the children—but also areas that are not as apparent—those that might get hit later. Some of your life will be washed away and "lost at sea" such as:

◇ Financial security, or the ability to get a loan or purchase needed items

◇ Your credit standing and the opportunity to obtain a loan or appropriate or affordable health insurance

◇ Even little things that still cause continued grief: your favorite furniture or vegetable garden you spent years tending

If you are forced to move, you and your children may lose:

◇ Friends and neighbors

◇ The woman who walks her dog each morning and stops to say hi to you

◇ Close relationship with the postman, store clerks, and other community members

◇ School friends and favorite teachers or sports coaches

◇ Church friends and "family" or your favorite pastor

The list can go on. Some of these things are big, some small. All will require a certain period of grieving as you continue to let go.

Divorce's nuclear fallout

The waiting period after divorce is marked by both rebuilding and the danger of more problems that can surface. After the earthquake in Japan, the next big danger that awaited the victims of the tsunami was a possible nuclear power plant explosion and radiation poisoning. Like the effects of the monster waves, radiation was feared to be making its way across the ocean to the California coast. The effects of divorce also continue to be far reaching. Just when you start to rebuild and feel a little better, you may face "fallout":

- ◇ The kids, who seemed to have been adjusting, are now failing school
- ◇ Your teens begin to take drugs or have sex
- ◇ Your children want to go live with their other parent
- ◇ Your adult children take sides and stop talking to you
- ◇ Your ex is now dating someone you used to know
- ◇ Your ex-husband's girlfriend or new wife just got pregnant
- ◇ The bank finally called in the note on the house
- ◇ Your company fires you because of all the stress you'd brought to work

⬦ Your ex moves and you lose touch with the kids

When you become radioactive

Global shipping companies in Japan refused to dock near the Fukushima nuclear power plant, instead rerouting to other seaports of Japan that seemed safer from radioactivity.

After divorce there are people who used to be friendly to you but who now see you as some kind of "radioactive" pariah who should be avoided. They stop talking to you and inviting you to their parties, and they walk quickly the other way when they see you coming. They don't want your radioactive poison!

> After divorce there are people who used to be friendly to you but who now see you as some kind of "radioactive" pariah who should be avoided.

Maybe you can relate to these comments by divorced men and women who wrote to me about their nuclear fallout:

> My sister-in-law and I were best friends. We even had our babies the same week. We did everything together. I just can't believe that after

the divorce she took her brother's side. At first I was angry, then depressed. In a way, that hurt me as much as my husband walking out on me.

—*Sheila*

My mother-in-law loved me. After the divorce, she was very kind to me, but something eventually began to happen. Slowly she stopped coming by for visits, even with her grandkids. I haven't seen her for months, and she missed the twins' birthday. She never did that before.

—*Maryanne*

When I was married, it was the wives who made sure we had a social life. Most of our friends were my ex-wife's girlfriends and their husbands, and I thought I was pretty close to those guys. All of our kids went to the same Catholic elementary school, and we were all in the same parish. After the divorce I assumed they would still invite me to the guys' gatherings. It didn't happen. I was actually shocked when I found out from our kids that my ex and her new boyfriend were at the big annual block party that I used to attend. I guess I was naïve.

—*Bob*

I worked for my ex's father. He fired me after the divorce. "Sorry to let you go, Jim. But I know you understand." Now she wants even more child support. Go figure.

—*Jim*

I never thought I'd lose our home. Ever. He knew the kids grew up there and we all loved it. He had plenty of money, but he forced the sale of the house.

—*Jackie*

Well, you never know who your real friends are. After a while, people at our church quit talking to me. Church! Can you believe that?

—*Anonymous*

Aftershocks!

When a tragedy such as an undersea earthquake and tsunami hit, the worst may not be over—there are always aftershocks. Japan's aftershocks were rated at between 6.0 and 7.0 levels, enough on their own to cause serious subsequent damage. Part of rebuilding after divorce is moving past any naïveté and being ready for the aftershocks that *will* come. In post-traumatic stress mode (that can linger for years), those who rebuild after divorce can fall into what some call mythical thinking—false hopes and a refusal to accept reality. Those kinds of thoughts keep us stuck in rigid ways of thinking, and they make us buckle under stress. Instead, accepting reality makes us much more flexible when the aftershocks of divorce hit. Your ex-spouse, the courts, or others involved may be cooperative one day, attacking the next. Pray that that doesn't happen, but be smart enough to expect aftershocks after things begin to settle down. Be prepared. If you can relate to some of the comments following, you may be stuck in mythical thinking that keeps you from rolling with the punches.

I just can't believe that after all he took from us, now he wants the house, too!

I'm in shock! She said she'd never try to go for spousal support. Today I got served with a summons for nearly half my paycheck!

I never imagined in a million years that this divorce would still be going on. It's been three years and he's still fighting me in court.

I can't believe it—she is refusing to let me see my kids now.

Wake up. More waves may be bound to hit, even years later, when college tuition is due or the kids get married and can't be at both your houses on Christmas Day.

Divorce is both tragedy and hope

People magazine's headline reads "Tragedy and Hope," with a beautiful subheading that we can apply to the post-divorce period: "A historic 9.0 earthquake . . . washes away whole coastal cities—but not people's determination to overcome the physical and psychological aftershocks."[1]

When I asked divorced people to share what they eventually learned in the aftermath and the waiting period, this is what they told me.

> I learned how to grieve the loss of the friendship with my sister-in-law. I realized that over time it mattered less and less to me. Now I feel sorry for her. She was put in a difficult position too and felt she had to make a choice. It took a while, but I have a new friend now. And you know what? I will appreciate this relationship more and not take it for granted.
>
> —*Sheila*

> I was angry at my ex-mother-in-law not just for abandoning me but her grandkids. But I waited for God to restore that hole in our life. I read in Scripture that God comforts the widows and orphans. In a way, the divorce made me a widow and the kids orphans. For months I clung to that verse and waited. It was a long

wait—two years. Then we got a new next-door neighbor, and she has become the most loving substitute grandmother to the kids. And she loves me too.

—*Maryanne*

After divorce I used the waiting period to analyze what I had done wrong and what I could do better to rebuild my life. I admitted that I had taken the lazy way out, in a certain sense, by letting the wives take charge of the social life and all my friendships. Even though I was uninvited to all the old events, there was one couple on our street who stayed friends with me. The guy really reached out to me and had me and the boys over for barbecues. I guess I'd say in the waiting your true friends will be revealed in a way that they might not have otherwise. And that's a good thing that comes in the waiting.

—*Bob*

I waited for the right job to come along after my father-in-law fired me. I asked God to help me not rush into anything and to wait for His guidance. At first I got an offer I almost took, but because I refused to be anxious and reactive, I got a call from an old friend who wanted to open our own business together. We'd been pals since high school, and now I am making money and enjoying my work like I never have before. Wait and trust. The waiting is hard. So's the trust. But just do it.

—Jim

We're renting now, and it's been almost three years. I can't believe I'm admitting this: I am so relieved to be out from under the huge burden of a home mortgage and all the maintenance that goes with it. I loved that house, but I love the peace and ease and the lack of stress in our lives. The kids are even happier. I'm waiting to see if it's even smart to try to buy again in the near future. Who knows? In the waiting I'm just enjoying where we live right now.

—Jackie

So remember, recovery and rebuilding takes time—but it's worth the wait. Don't rush it.

Chapter 10

Don't Rush the Process

FOUR days after the Japan earthquake, I was in line for morning coffee and a bear claw when I saw a *USA Today* headline that perfectly described another aftermath of divorce: "An Anxious Wait." The waiting period after an initial hit and the aftershocks can seem like forever. That's when you have to get in the habit of reminding yourself it's *not* forever. It just feels like it. One of the biggest problems of waiting to rebuild the right way is that the anxiety can set some divorced people up for rushing into new relationships.

We are already a culture who does not like to wait for anything, and divorce can make us even more anxious!

We are already a culture who does not like to wait for anything, and divorce can make us even more anxious! I still can get caught up in the rush that seduces us all, and I can fall into the trap of always seeming to be in a hurry for something. One of my pet peeves is waiting for someone who is dawdling along, walking slower than I am and falling far behind me. (If you are that person, can't you please pick it up a bit? Come on!) We can't wait for our tax return, summer vacation, or Christmas Eve. And what about the church parking lot? Would it kill you to wait and let a few other cars go ahead of you?

How long until I'm healed or ready to date?

Phyllis is on *The Catholic's Divorce Survival Guide* DVD series—the woman who says, "I made a big mistake. I rushed into a relationship. . . . It wasn't fair to me, and it wasn't fair to him. I needed a year or two to figure out who I was." Recently Phyllis told me, "A year or two? Ha! I should have made that four or five years."

After divorce, many people can't wait for someone new to come into their life and make them feel valuable, attractive, or loved again. They have a very high level of anxiety.

"I just need to be with an opposite-sex friend so I can feel better about myself."

"I only want to know that I still have what it takes. What's wrong in that?"

In hearing the stories of men and women in my

divorce recovery groups, I've discovered these facts to be true:

Dating is never casual. I hear people rationalize that their dating is only casual, as if that makes it okay to rush into a relationship. But people's hearts and hopes are involved! You could be using—the opposite of loving—each other to fill lonely places in your life. Are you playing with fire? Don't take a chance of burning your house down again.

"A year or two" is not long enough for anyone to fully heal and be ready to enter a new relationship. You might *feel* better in six months or a year, but that does not mean you *are* better—or ready to give yourself wholly and completely to another. The annulment process itself—required for Catholics who want to remarry—may take that long or longer, and what if you don't have grounds for one?

If you start dating and are not fully ready to remarry, you set the other person up for a deeply wounded heart. That's not loving. As the saga of the tsunami continued across daily newspapers, the latest reports centered on a large moving mass of debris—houses, cars, and even human body parts—that was headed to the California coast. Damaged emotions of fear, anger, betrayal—and more—all need plenty of time to heal. It is not loving to bring all that flotsam and jetsam to another person's life.

Depth of the relationship will determine the time.

I remember some in my divorce groups who admitted they were hurt by the divorce but were not as terribly wounded or as devastated as others in the group appeared. They wondered why. As the weeks went on the answer appeared: they had never been fully engaged or deeply committed in their marriages in the first place, even if the marriage had lasted five years or fifty. Some people love their spouse and children but live their life at a surface level. They occupy their days and nights with routines of work, rearing children, light conversation, and weekly or monthly sex as if those were all simply the things you do. They never develop a mature interior life or go to deep emotional levels in their marriages or maybe any of their relationships. As a result, when it's over, they are shaken but not to the core. For those who were deeply attached, had the higher hopes, and had been the most fully committed, the wounds will seem greater and the time to heal will be longer.

A high anxiety for new love can push us into unhealthy, if not sinful, relationships. As in the recovery period in Japan, military troops will be mobilized, volunteers will move in, and rebuilding will happen—but reconstruction will take a long time, maybe many years. The same is true with divorce. If you try to rush it, you're bound to suffer a relapse. You'll also build a new home that will collapse again when the next big wave hits.

Ask God for patience. Then ask Him the next day too. Eventually the dust will settle. The noise and confusion *will s*top. Here are some things to do in the waiting period:

Pray

Why do we always leave prayer for last when it should be first? And not only first, but steadily throughout the days and nights.

> Prayer was the ONLY thing I had time for.
> —*Barb*

When you're too tired to pray, or you forget, ask the Holy Spirit to pray to the Father for you. He will!

Allow yourself to grieve

That includes whining, crying, isolation, and periods of letting yourself feel blue. But don't do it alone or it can become self-pity. Take Christ with you into those dark places and dump it all on Him. Be real. Then don't allow yourself to stay there too long. Healthy grieving is necessary. Indulgent grief can be a sin.

Look around for new friendships

Wash your face, put on a clean shirt, and go out into the world. Force yourself to say "Hi" (even when you don't feel like it) to that new grocery store clerk. Stop putting off registering in the new parish and stay after Mass for coffee.

Let your hands be empty

During the waiting period as you rebuild, catch your feelings of panic or anxiety if you can't find new friends or the things you lost. You don't need all those new things yet.

Do first things first

While you're waiting for life to get back to "normal" (whatever that was!), make sure you're giving the limited time and energy you have to the most important things: God first, then the kids, then others. You get to be first only if you have serious emotional or health issues that need attention.

Practice patience

I once lived in a house that had some pretty shoddy workmanship. The basic structure was sound; however, there were many, many areas of the house that needed to be redone. Over a period of years, with much patience, a lot of elbow grease, and funds as they became available, the house began to take shape. The house turned out beautifully and has received numerous accolades.

—*Marlene*

Your life after divorce can turn out beautifully too, but only if you can learn to be intentional about being patient. Whenever I get anxious or frustrated with how long things might be taking, I practice the presence of God. I simply say, "Come, Lord," and I imagine Him right next to me. Sometimes He's quiet; sometimes He speaks to my heart. Often it seems He just looks at me and shakes His head and smiles. It helps.

Go to a grief or divorce group

Jeff really opened up about what he did during his post-divorce waiting and reconstruction period:

> Looking back, I think attending divorce recovery classes or doing a one-day intensive seminar, like I did a few years ago, is a critical step to rebuilding one's life . . . because we have no other organized way to confront our pain, deal with the emotions, address the tough questions, and build a plan to move forward. . . .
>
> I found that I simply did not want to deal with the emotional aftermath of my divorce. It was painful, and many aspects of what happened made me very angry with my ex, so angry that it was hard for me to see even my own responsibility for the situation. I was the one who married her, even though there were many warning signs [that what I was doing wasn't right]. . . .
>
> After the divorce, I found that moments of sadness, grief, and anger would sweep over me

at different times, often unexpectedly, and force me to think about things I didn't want to think about. But the thing I liked about having the intensive divorce recovery seminar was the fact that it forced me to set aside a day to deal with some of these emotions and issues that were never convenient to deal with through the normal course of my daily routine.

Fact is, you have to spend time assessing what went wrong, why it went wrong, what God's plan is for you in life, and where you are going to go from here. If you don't commit some time to reflection, therapy, and getting your bearings, you might fall into another trap or make another mistake.

I also found great solace in sharing my experiences with other divorcees in the seminar. Just hearing their experiences were therapeutic for me because they made me realize that I wasn't alone, that I wasn't being singled out, and, perhaps more importantly, that I wasn't a bad person.

I also think the seminar . . . helps you rebuild your self esteem and create a fresh start for the next half of your life. So, in the step-by-step order of things to do on rebuilding one's life, I think attending a day-long divorce seminar or series of classes would be high on the list. You

need to do this because if you don't, you probably won't dedicate as much time and thought
as you should to understanding your divorce and
creating a new foundation for your life moving
forward.

Great words of advice on what to do in the waiting period after a divorce. Jeff is a beautiful example of
taking his time to do it right. You can see and hear him
tell more of his story on *The Catholic's Divorce Survival
Guide* DVD series.

Chapter 11

Clear Your Title

IF you bought a residential lot and were building a new home, you could never get a construction loan without the proper paperwork. The bank wants to know who you are, how much money you make, how much savings you have, and what debts you carry. After exhaustive inquiry into your most private finances, the bank may finally clear you for the loan. But they also require a title report, another investigative legal process that makes sure before you close escrow that the property you want to buy is indeed free and clear—no prior owner still has any ownership interest in where you want to live.

In this rebuilding analogy, your former spouse may be likened to a prior owner who may or may not have a legitimate sacramental claim on you. Even if you feel the marriage is over, you may not be as free and clear as you think. Every divorced Catholic needs to ask the question, what does the Catholic Church have to say about my marital status? This is the time to start thinking about your standing in the Church. Are you really single? Or are you still married? Who decides? Maybe you've asked yourself the following:

◇ Do I even want to marry again?
◇ Is my marriage still valid in the eyes of the Church?
◇ Do I have grounds for an annulment?
◇ What *is* an annulment anyway?

Marriage is the foundation of our civilization and carries great moral, social, and spiritual significance—who is married to whom determines our entire future! Marriage is not just a social construct or a civil right to be demanded by anyone; it comes directly from God. This sacred relationship has been under severe attack in recent times and is misunderstood by many, even good Catholics. I never really understood the Church's teachings on divorce and annulments until I first began to understand marriage. When I discovered the beauty and truth of Church teachings, I was shocked and delighted at the same time. I thought, *I never knew that! Why didn't someone ever tell me these things?*

So let's start at the beginning. I wrote a book entitled *Understanding and Petitioning for Your Decree of Nullity*,[1] which I highly recommend you read. But let's briefly summarize with a simple Q&A format in this chapter:

What is marriage?

It's the loving relationship between one man and one woman who are free and able to say "I do" to a permanent ('til death), exclusive (no one else), and faithful (in every way) union that is never intentionally closed off to the gift of new life. In short, it is a *free, full, faithful,* and *fruitful* union of love.

Why did God give us marriage?

It's a sign that points us to Him and His love for us. In a certain sense, God Himself is a *free, full, faithful,* and *fruitful* PERFECT exchange of love between the Persons in the Holy Trinity. We were created to get caught up into that love and enjoy it with Him forever. We can first experience something of that eternal joy in our earthly marriage. By tasting the goodness of a loving marriage on earth, God desires that we hunger for the endless fulfillment of such Love: Him.

What is the purpose of marriage?

Very simply put, to unite the couple in authentic love that blesses and binds them to each other and to bring about new life into the world. The Church calls these the *unitive* and *procreative* aspects of marriage.

Because of sin, families can and do get damaged, but from the beginning God always intended that having a natural mom and dad loving each other in the same home is the best place for children to grow and thrive. The union of love and life must never be intentionally separated, because these two mirror God Himself, who is inseparable and perfect *Love* and *Life*.

Why did Jesus call Himself the Bridegroom?

God desires a permanent and loving union with every human soul forever—a mystical marriage with Him. That's why we're here. After Adam and Eve's fall, Jesus came as the Bridegroom to rescue, woo, and win the hearts of those who would open up to receive Him. He prepares a home for us with Him in Heaven. *That's* the happily-ever-after we all really want, whether we realize it or not! Thus, by looking to the qualities of Christ's love for us, the Church determines what makes a true marriage. It's one that has the capacity to be *free*, *full*, *faithful*, and *fruitful*.

What is a Sacrament?

It's an outward action we do that mystically unites us in an intimate union with Jesus, particularly in His loving and life-giving act of dying on the Cross, conquering sin, and restoring new life. A Sacrament has both a visible (earthly) component and invisible (heavenly) one. In baptism, for example, we have the visible water as the sign to cleanse the soul and give it spiritual life and invisible words that invite the Holy Spirit into the act to make the sign a reality. Sacraments always have both visible and invisible elements because Jesus Himself is the marriage (union) of the human and the divine—Heaven and earth, God and man, visible and invisible. In marriage, the outward visible action is the two spouses giving consent when they say "I do." Those words have the power to lift their love up into the heavens and put it on spiritual steroids!

Why is marriage a Sacrament?

Because, entered into rightly, it unites the spouses on earth with Jesus in Heaven. The married couple becomes "one" not just with each other but as part of the mystical marriage of Jesus and His Bride. There are powerful, life-giving graces that flow from the marriage of Jesus and His Bride (the Church), and marriage allows couples to share in and drink deeply from the well of those special graces. And who doesn't want all the help they can get to have the best—and holiest—marriage possible?

Why is a valid marriage unbreakable?

If a marriage is valid, it mirrors and gets caught up into that unbreakable bond between Jesus and the Church. His loving vow to be our "spouse" will never break. He promised He would never fail us or forsake us.[2] Thus, a valid marriage bond can never be broken.

> If a marriage is valid, it mirrors and gets caught up into that unbreakable bond between Jesus and the Church.

That's why there is no such thing as a Catholic divorce. There is only the process whereby the Church declares that there may have been a wedding but there never was a valid marriage bond to begin with (the Decree of Nullity). Divorce refers only to the civil marriage.

Was my marriage a valid marriage?

I know it was your marriage—and no one knows what went on in it better than you—but please don't presume that you know the answer.

Feeling (and hoping and even trying very hard!) that you were validly married doesn't mean you were. And even if you had the right intent and full capacity for marriage as the Church intends, perhaps your spouse did not. Maybe you didn't realize that.

Just in the little you've read preceding, perhaps you can see that what constitutes a valid or invalid marriage is a complex issue and one that the average lay person doesn't fully understand. I know I certainly didn't until I sought an annulment. I learned even more when I was trained by my diocese to serve as a lay advocate to assist those going through the process.

A valid marriage bond takes place when both the bride and groom enter into it with the right intent and the full capacity to marry. In other words, you must really know what marriage requires and be able to live it out. People with severe psychological or emotional problems, those with addictions, or those who are extremely immature or naïve may desire marriage but not be able to fully give the goods of marriage to a spouse.

If you or your spouse reserved divorce as a possible option (something increasingly common) or considered an affair permissible under certain circumstances, then a true marriage bond may not have been created. Perhaps the words "I do" were exchanged, but something else in the head or heart invalidated them.

How can the Church make that decision?

The Church is the true Bride of Christ. Her Bridegroom, Jesus Christ, gave Her the keys to the family car and put Her name on his bank account, just like my father did with my mother. Mom had Dad's full authority over us through her marriage to him. They were one!

So too the Church is our Mother and can take a look at what went on at the time we said "I do" and see what was there—or not.

When you said "I do," was there something there (an out-of-wedlock pregnancy that caused grave fear and pressure) or something missing (one or both of you refused to be open to children) that rendered your consent invalid? In the annulment process—where the Church may issue a Decree of Nullity—you work with the local Church tribunal to determine if there is cause for invalidity.

What are the grounds for an annulment?

There are many specific ways marital consent could have been invalid. A valid marriage has to be intended to and able to mirror that marriage between Jesus and the Church:

◊ His love and commitment to us are FREE of fear, pressure, or agendas.

◊ His vows to us are FULL, meaning He gives all of Himself to only us forever, nothing ever held back. Even to the point of death on a cross.

◇ His intent is to be completely FAITHFUL to us in every way, all the time.
◇ His union with us is FRUITFUL, causing us to be filled with new divine life.

This is exactly what the Catholic Church wedding vows must proclaim: that we come here *freely*, to give ourselves to each other *fully*, being *faithful* in every way, and being *fruitful* and open to the gift of life. If at least one person did not or could not make such vows, no true marriage bond was created.

What happens if I get a Decree of Nullity?

Your marriage bond will be publicly (within the Church) declared invalid, and you are free to attempt marriage again, if you so choose, within the Church and according to Her requirements.

Are my children declared illegitimate?

Never! The Church recognizes all the good that came from an attempted marriage, including genuine affection, shared life, and the beauty and dignity of your children. The term *illegitimate* was originally a civil term and first intended to help settle property disputes between heirs. The Church is concerned only with your personhood, not your property.

Where do I start with the annulment process?

Begin with your local pastor or seek the counsel of another wise and holy priest. They are trained to help you. And by all means, educate yourself as much as possible on the process so you are not led down some path you do not want to—or should not—go down.

Why do I need an annulment?

If you don't plan to remarry, you don't need one. But if you truly believe you had an invalid marriage, or suspect you may have, and want the closure this may bring, do proceed with the investigation. Until you do and the Church grants you a Decree of Nullity, you are still married to your ex-spouse in the eyes of the Church.

How can men at the tribunal invade the privacy of our marriage and declare it null?

This was the question that was posed to me at a recent divorce recovery event. The woman who asked was recently divorced, and I saw deep pain on her face and heard it in her voice. "I *know* my marriage was valid!" she said. First, I affirmed her sense of anger and wanting to protect what was private. Then I shared that it is not only men who serve on the tribunal; many smart and holy Catholic women are canon lawyers, judges, and advocates. I used the analogy of going to the doctor for a stomach pain that would not go away. You know you do not have a tumor. It's your body. You don't feel like there is a tumor. But you sacrifice privacy and submit yourself to the doctor's pokes, probes, and other embarrassments to solve the problem of the pain. Yes, it's your body, but they are trained professionals (and you are not). And when they take blood tests and X-rays and discover a tumor, no one accuses or blames you. In a similar way, those at the tribunal do not judge you; they are only there to find the truth, the problem of the pain. Then they help you accept the results.

I told the woman that if she would submit to the process, two things would happen: (1) with a negative decision, she would have a trained team affirm that there was not enough evidence to support invalidity. She would then not be alone in her desire and decision to live as a separate but still married woman. That's a tough cross to bear, and no one should carry it alone. Or (2) she could begin to more fully understand what really happened when she and her former spouse married and how the Church could help her rebuild a life with new possibilities—if she so chose. Most who have gone through the process agree they learned a lot they thought they knew, but did not.

Can I get married again?

Not if you are still married. That's adultery. Only when and if you obtain a Decree of Nullity are you free to attempt marriage again within the Church. You should not even *think* about dating anyone else—even for that little "cup of coffee"—until you have taken care of your marital status in the Church. Why? Not only to protect the private and public dimensions of the presumed-valid marriage bond—which affects the whole community—but for the sake of the other person. Ask anyone who has fallen in love again after a divorce and had to wait for an annulment—or worse, not gotten one. It puts incredible stress and strain on the parties and tempts them to unchastity. That is simply not loving. If you truly care about someone, take the high road. Don't use another person to quell your loneliness or build up your self-esteem after a divorce. That's selfish—and sinful. Pray about this.

What if the Church denies me an annulment?

Then you have been given a great gift from God—a cross to bear as He bore His for you. We forget the blessings and virtues that can come to us in suffering done rightly. Talk to your pastor or another wise and holy priest to see what to do after a negative decision from the local marriage tribunal. It's not the end of the world. The Church upholds justice but is full of compassion and mercy too.

What if I have already remarried outside the Church?

Go talk to that pastor or wise-and-holy-priest to whom I keep sending you! It sounds a little like a digestion problem, but you are in what the Church calls an "irregular" marriage—that is, it did not follow the form that would bring about a valid marriage bond and the graces of a Sacrament. If you didn't get an annulment, you are presumed still married. Now living as married in another union, you're technically committing adultery.

I know that sounds harsh! But like a good parent, the Church only wants the very best for you in every way. In Her wisdom She knows what needs to be done to help you live as Christ intends. Do you have to leave the new spouse? Not necessarily. But you may have to stop living as married until the prior marriage is found to be invalid. Don't panic and don't give up. God's grace is extremely powerful and *with Him* all things are possible.[3] Go talk to that priest!

Can I still go to Communion?

Divorced Catholics may go to Communion if they are not remarried outside the Church and not in the state of mortal sin. The divorce itself does not put you outside the Church. It's a serious sin that keeps us away from that intimate encounter with our Lord. Was sin involved in the breakup of the marriage? Then confess it and be free.

The word *communion* has great significance—it means that those who receive Communion are in communion with Christ and His Bride, the Church, and all that He has given Her the authority to teach. The outward act should be consistent with the inner heart of a man or woman. Thus, anyone who is not in full communion with the Church is asked to refrain from an act that makes them appear to be in full communion. That's why non-Catholics do not go to Communion with us—they are not in full communion with us. An outward act that seems to be untrue can cause confusion and scandal and should be avoided out of love for the rest of the community.

> The annulment process may be able to help you clear up matters and return you to full communion.

Have you remarried outside the Church? Then you are still Catholic, still very much part of the Church family, and deeply loved, but you have gone outside what the Church has said is best for you and are no longer in full communion. She wants you to be back in full graces, but there is work to be done. Until then, your Mother the Church asks that you not present yourself for Communion, for it would be hypocritical to receive Communion when one is not in full communion with the Church. The annulment process may be able to help you clear up matters and return you to full communion. If you encounter difficulties, please find a wise and holy priest to assist you.

No matter how long you may find yourself outside of full communion, can you still make a spiritual communion with Christ? Yes! Every moment of every day if you wish.

What others have to say

No one wants to look in the mirror and see flaws. After divorce, some people deeply resent having anyone dig into their private lives, especially their painful past. They already may feel violated, attacked, wounded, and vulnerable from their divorce. In divorce and its aftermath, self-esteem can take a huge hit! If these men and women don't have a sensitive pastor or another trained person to advocate for them during the process, it can close their hearts to the gifts that invariably come from an open and honest look at their life and marriage. But the annulment process has tremendous capacity for emotional healing and spiritual growth.

After my divorce, I forced myself to take action in areas that I knew I needed to address. MOST, most important, I went through the annulment process. Very important for me to do. This was strictly for ME.

—*Stacy*

I had to take a good, hard look at my life and why and how I entered the marriage. It was painful, and I had to admit many of my own character defects and weaknesses. But it felt good at the same time, like looking at how you've been eating and admitting you're fifty pounds overweight from drinking beer and eating all those French fries over the years. In the annulment process, you can see what happened and find new ways to live and love again so you never have to get on that "scale" again!

—*Jack*

My advocate really helped me be honest in a way that I never had before. The questions they asked were straightforward, and you could tell they made a lot of sense in seeing if the marriage bond was valid or not. I learned so much about myself, my ex, the Church teachings, and how marriage is supposed to be from going through the annulment.

—*Enrique*

I was a regular churchgoer before but could not participate fully in my faith. The annulment process has given me that. And some very interesting asides came out of that . . . a lot of introspection from my brother (who was there with me in our extremely abusive childhood) and a much closer relationship. It was a painful process however, I cannot say enough about it. It was personally enlightening and, surprisingly, had a profound effect on those who were asked to participate in being a witness for me.

—*P. R.*

Don't be afraid. It's worth it.

—*Mark*

What next?

So far in your rebuilding, I presume you have done (or will do) the following:

- ◇ Begun to really let go of people, places, or things to which you have been too attached
- ◇ Gotten to understand something of God's infinite love for you and the true home He has prepared for you in Heaven
- ◇ Decided to make eternity (not the here and now) your foundation and make Christ the cornerstone of your new life

◇ Gone to the Church "Title Company" to
clear up matters of your marital status

If so, now you are ready to dig more deeply into
the practical areas of your life, starting with fencing off
the construction zone while you rebuild. Neighbor's
dogs, pesky critters, and even nosy neighbors will begin
to intrude into your life as you start to make changes.
Everyone will want to know what is going on with you,
so you'll need some healthy boundaries.

Chapter 12

Erect Sturdy Boundaries

My sister Barb shared a story about a weak, wooden fence in her backyard.

> The neighbors' growling, biting, angry pit bull broke through the wood fence one day when I was babysitting an eighteen-month-old in the backyard. I grabbed the kid, ran in the house, and bolted the door.
>
> Afterward, I tried to plan what to do in the event it happened again. A retired cop friend of mine told me I should take my gun out with me whenever I was in the yard and just empty it into the dog if it broke through again. I didn't want to do that but didn't know what else to do.
>
> Every morning when I went out on the patio to have my coffee and read my newspaper, the dog would pace back and forth along the fence, stopping and snarling at me as it reached each end of the yard. Back and forth, growling and

growling. I just started saying, in a very friendly, sing-song voice: "Good morning, dog! How are you? Isn't it a nice day? Good morning." Every single time I saw that damned dog, I'd start my sing-song again. I prayed for it. I sang "happy" down its throat whenever I saw it and prayed again. I pasted a smile on my face and kept sing-songing. And one day the dog stopped growling—for good. Ha ha ha ha!

After divorce, you might have to sing "happy" down the throat of someone who keeps threatening or making your life miserable. And you know who I mean!

Everyone needs boundaries

Part of rebuilding means finding the weak spots where problems can come into your life and cause emotional, spiritual, financial, or even physical harm. You'll need to build strong walls that the strong winds can't blow down and where the rain can't seep in. You have to both plan ahead and have a solid structure. At a divorce conference recently, a woman

> You'll need to build strong walls that the strong winds can't blow down and where the rain can't seep in.

admitted to me and the group that she always hated "rules and regs" and would do anything not to have to obey. "I feel controlled and resentful," she shared. More than a few heads nodded in agreement. I explained that that is a common response when one feels they can't trust the maker of the rules to meet their needs. "If your parents simply issued orders, never explained the 'why' behind the rules, and ignored who you were as a person, you probably resent authority."

"Yes!" she said, laughing, and then became serious. "I had a lot of abuse in my childhood and never did feel that my parents were truly looking out for me. Sometimes I feel that way about the Church. The whole issue of having to stay within boundaries is confining. The word *structure* sounds like prison to me!"

Some people think personal boundaries—protective walls—are not a good thing because they shut you off from the world. It's true that some walls are erected for self-protection but can become more like prison walls. I recently moved to Marin County in California, where the famous San Quentin Prison is only a mile or so away. I'm glad they have thick, concrete walls, iron gates with bolts, alarms, and armed guards. With prison walls, the person behind them can't be reached, nor do they reach out to others. But it's not the wall (boundary that you set) that is right or wrong; it's the motivation *behind it* that can be healthy or harmful. What, or who, are you trying to keep out and why?

Here are some examples of healthy boundaries after a divorce:

◇ When friends ask what happened, be careful with whom you share. Don't always tell all the sordid details of the divorce. For many, it's not their business, so keep them out. Save that for your therapist, doctor, or spiritual director—do invite *them* in.

◇ If the kids (even the adult children) want to know why Mom or Dad did this or that, keep it simple and maybe even keep out of it. Inappropriate information is not their business or their responsibility.

◇ If you want to know about your ex, keep the kids out of the middle. Don't make them your personal messengers; it creates such conflict in their hearts and can teach them to play both sides. You can invite yourself in to your former spouse's life by making direct and clear contact.

◇ If your ex grills your children for information, teach your children to keep themselves out of the middle. "Dad, Mom said if you want to know, you should talk to her."

◇ Don't share your personal financial information with the children or anyone. (It's not their business.) Keep them out, but do invite your attorney or accountant in.

◇ If family members want to get overly involved in any way, keep them out.

◇ And if *you* are dying to pry into your ex's life, keep your nose out!

◇ If the ex inappropriately tries to intrude into your relationship with your children, learn kind but firm ways to keep him or her out.

◇ If you haven't cleared up your marital status through the annulment process, keep dating out.

◇ If you start dating, keep chastity in and immorality out. Time alone with a date and a bottle of wine while the kids are at their other parent's house for the weekend may definitely have to be out. It always starts out innocent but can be almost impossible to handle. Double dating and group events are better to have in.

◇ If you start dating, keep him or her out for a long time until you are sure this may lead to a sacramental marriage.

◇ If your new romantic interest has children, be protective of their hearts too. Keep family intimacy (going to the zoo, parks, movies, and even church together) out until you two are seriously considering marriage.

◇ If you're at that point in a serious courtship, keep sleeping over out; keep good example for the kids in.

There's a lot more, but that should get you started in the right direction.

Difficulty setting and enforcing boundaries

Some people just can't set a healthy boundary. Others can, but they won't bring themselves to enforce it. Do you tell your children that if they don't do the dinner dishes they will not get to watch TV? When they ignore you, do you simply let it go and heave a huge sigh? Worse, do you do the dishes for them? If so, it's fear that might be holding you back.

You might be afraid of being a bad person

You may not set or follow through on a good boundary because you don't want to be seen as mean, selfish, unchristian, or even a bad person. Having people think well of you can be a drug-like intoxication to the ego. Sometimes feeling good about ourselves usurps precedence over doing the difficult or right thing—which includes enforcing a good boundary. If the culture says we need to be nice, we may actually end up tolerating abuse. The culture has lied to us about what it means to be a good person or a good parent; it's the Church that has the truth. Jesus was not always "nice"—He got angry at the hypocrites, called them on their sinfulness, and talked hard and tough to their trickery. Start reading Scripture. In the next section we'll look to see how Jesus was very skilled at setting and enforcing healthy (and holy!) boundaries.

You might be afraid of causing conflict

You might not set or follow through on a good boundary because you hate conflict. Some temperaments crave peace at any cost. They just do not like to deal with conflict, so they don't. After divorce, this can most frequently appear in the relationships within the family. Some divorced parents fear further upsetting their children, who may have become the center of the family. If your kids have become somewhat narcissistic (me, me, me!), then you know upsetting them could cause a tsunami of its own! But trading their holiness for your peace can cause your kids to eventually drown in their own selfishness. Don't fail to hold them to higher ways of living.

And who else may be pushing your buttons, disrespecting you, or causing problems? Are you letting others walk all over you? Your kids are watching. What are they learning from you?

You might be afraid of losing love, loyalty, and affection

You might not set or follow through on a good boundary because you fear rejection. It feels so good to have someone—be it the kids, your ex, or someone else—love, admire, or appreciate us that we don't want to risk losing it. That fear of loss enslaves us to them, and we will be afraid to hold them to higher standards, call them to accountability, or otherwise be in an authentic and loving relationship with them. When that happens, we are not really loving them rightly; we are using them to feed our insecurities or our egos.

If someone has been pushing you to the limit and you struggle with boundaries, ask God to show you how to handle the situation. Talk it over with your therapist, spiritual director, or any wise and holy person who might be able to help. You may need to be quiet and accept it—or you may need to open your mouth, state the truth, and stand your ground. Like Jesus.

When Jesus set—and enforced—boundaries

It's a false religion that says if we say no to someone that we are being unkind and, even worse, unchristian. At the center of this false Christianity is the pretty Jesus, one who is ever-smiling, soft and gentle, and sweet and sappy. He is so loving that He never says no to anyone.

This fake Jesus is supremely tolerant of everyone and everything, would never judge, and always turns the other cheek. *Scre-e-e-e-ech!* Hold it right there! That is not the true Jesus, and you will not find Him in Scripture. If you are to rebuild your life with Jesus as the cornerstone and to follow His lead, you'd better start to know who He really is.

He didn't care what others thought of Him

Jesus wasn't a slave to what others thought about Him. He was fully aware of how much He was loved by and one with the Father. He didn't need others' approval. Because He was free from fear of rejection, He could confidently and fearlessly call everyone to a place of personal holiness. We need to be the same—in union with God and free from worry of what others think—in order to set healthy boundaries for ourselves and others.

He is not tolerant . . . of sin

Tolerance and political correctness are two current buzzwords of our culture's false religion. You do not have to, and should not ever, tolerate what is wrong.

Jesus did not tolerate everyone, nor did he tolerate everything they did, said, or thought. Do you remember the story told in John 8:10–11, where there was a woman caught in the act of adultery? The townspeople had accused, judged, and condemned her to death by stoning right there in the street. They changed their minds when Jesus—who agreed the woman had sinned—said that whoever among them *without any sin* should be the first to throw a stone. They thought about it, were convicted of perhaps even deeper, darker sins of their own, dropped their rocks, and walked away.

Jesus looked up and said to her, "Woman, where are they? Has no one condemned you?"

She said, "No one, Lord."

And Jesus said, "Neither do I condemn you; go, and do not sin again."

Jesus did not *condemn*, but He did *judge* the situation. There's a difference. We're supposed to use our heads and judge between right and wrong. Jesus judged that her actions were sinful, and out of love for her eternal soul, He did not tolerate her choices. He lovingly admonished her, but in effect He also said, "Starting right now, stop it!"

He gets angry at sin

Jesus loves us and, yes, has a gentle side—but he also made a whip with His own hands, overturned tables, and drove the moneychangers out of the temple. They were abusing God's house and unjustly profiting from the poor. Jesus gets angry but does not sin. Anger at injustice should move us to corrective action as it did with Christ.

When Peter, whom Jesus dearly loved, suggested his Lord take the easy way out and avoid death on a cross, Jesus got angry with him and called him probably the nastiest name you can call a friend: "Satan." Your closest family or friends may encourage you to take an easy or selfish way out of a divorce-related problem. Don't call them Satan, but know that

> Your closest family or friends may encourage you to take an easy or selfish way out of a divorce-related problem.

the enemy is behind them as he was with Peter, whispering lies into their ears.

Jesus was also frequently angry with the arrogance of the Pharisees whom He called a "brood of vipers."[1] Today we might say, "You arrogant, self-righteous, low-life gutter snipes!" How gentle does *that* sound to you?

After divorce, when you're tempted to be greedy, selfish, or vengeful—or if someone is using, abusing, or taking unfair advantage of you—you have every right and perhaps the responsibility to refuse to participate in it. Say no.

He was not always available to everyone all the time

Scripture says Jesus was like us in every way except for sin. Like us, He could become utterly drained and exhausted after a full day of dealing with others' pain and problems. When you have emptied yourself for others, you need to be refilled with God's love. Jesus often shut down, went off by Himself somewhere far away from everyone (including his closest friends), and spent quiet time with His Father to rest and recharge. There were those He could have stayed and helped, but He did not. He set boundaries.

You might want to read chapter 5 in the Gospel of John, where Jesus once stopped by a large pool where there were many people who were sick, blind, lame, and paralyzed. He could have cured them all, but He did not and instead cured only one—a man who had been sick for thirty-eight years. Jesus told him to pick up his mat and go home. The man was cured, and he did go home. Some scholars tell us that Jesus knew curing physical ailments was a temporary healing of the body, but most important was that people believed in God and saved their souls. That one physical cure could have been the sign that cured the rest of the sick people at a much more important spiritual level.

In another Gospel story, crowds of people who were following Jesus swelled to the point that they were literally pressing in on Him. Some days He just couldn't take it any more—like a lot of us who are drained by the trauma of divorce and the demands of those who need us. So He took off!

But so much the more the report went abroad concerning him; and great multitudes gathered to hear and to be healed of their infirmities. But he withdrew to the wilderness and prayed.

—Luke 5:15–16

I think this shows overworked, stressed-out people who are trying to rebuild their lives after divorce. They need to focus their time and energy on the things that really matter, like quiet time with God the Father—resting in Him, opening to Him, and being united with Him. After I found some healing from God after divorce, I ran myself into exhaustion in divorce ministry because I wanted to save the world. I forgot that Jesus already did that! When you find yourself torn between many tasks or trying to help too many others, set some healthy boundaries and don't be afraid to back them up.

Say no to those of least importance and do the ones that unite you most closely with God. That's what the *real* Jesus did.

Setting boundaries

Here are some practical ways to put some structure and boundaries into your life.

Physical

Get rid of excess activity. Say no to unhealthy foods and too much wasted time. Start eating better. Turn off the TV, go to bed, and get up earlier. Get a calendar and pencil in time for exercise, even if it is a five-minute walk around the block. Start somewhere, but just do it. If you fail or forget, try again the next time. Get up and move, but get rest too. Setting bodily boundaries keeps you physically safe and healthy.

Emotional

In the twelve-step programs they tell you about H.A.L.T.—never let yourself get too *Hungry*, *Angry*, *Lonely*, or *Tired* or it will wreak havoc on your emotions. When our emotions are out of control, they are like lopsided laundry in the washer—clanging and banging and wearing down the motor. Emotions should be subject to our intellect and will. Tell yourself what you know: God is here to help. I'm not alone. "As it was in the beginning, is now, and ever shall be." It's all going to be okay! Setting boundaries with others keeps you emotionally safe.

Mental

We're pretty good at feeding our bodies and our emotions, but we need to feed our minds too. Your intellect needs to be fed with truth, not just the financial reports, society columns, or industry news that interests you. Those are good but can easily substitute for much more valuable, life-building, life-giving education. Get out your Catholic Bible, blow the dust off, put it in the open where you will see it every day, and when you walk by, stop and read something. Setting boundaries around how you spend your time and what you read keep you mentally safe and sound.

Spiritual

The Church sets a boundary for us: go to Mass at least once a week. The Mass is the most powerful prayer we have. Some people think that in the Mass Catholics keep crucifying Christ over and over, trying to get it right. They don't understand. We know that Jesus died once for all. But in a certain sense, each time we attend Mass we go outside time and space and mystically go to Calvary, where Jesus suffered, died, and rose again to conquer sin and overcome death. We don't crucify Him again and again; we go there again and again. Unlike Peter, who ran away, we get to stay at Calvary and offer our lives with Jesus to the Father. When the bread and wine are brought up to the altar to be "sacrificed" and changed, we offer ourselves to be changed. When we are united intimately with Christ, our own sinfulness gets nailed to the Cross and then we share in the glorious resurrection, filled with new life! This is mind-blowing stuff, folks, but from lack of teaching we can be utterly blinded—or blandly bored. Learn more about the Mass and what miraculous, mysterious, and mystical things happen every time. Setting a weekly boundary on your time to make sure you get to Mass and receive the Eucharist will keep you spiritually alive and well fed.

Sexual

Too often we have been told to say no to our sexual longings. I say it's time to say yes! Wait a minute, it's not what you think. We need to say yes to the greater, more beautiful plan God has for living and enjoying our true masculinity and femininity. Instead of saying yes to what the culture advises, we can say yes to God's much better plan. I discovered the truth of what it is to be a woman and to long for love in Pope John Paul II's biblical study about the theology of the body—how our bodies as male and female tell us something about God Himself.

> Setting sexual boundaries keeps you morally, emotionally, and physically safe.

One of the best introductory books I've read is *Theology of the Body for Teens.*[2] Don't let the name fool you. It's far from juvenile yet very easy to digest for all ages. I wrote how this changed my approach to sexuality in my conversion story in *Freedom: Twelve Lives Transformed by Theology of the Body.*[3] Setting sexual boundaries keeps you morally, emotionally, and physically safe.

Financial

Are you living on a budget? We all need structure in the area of finances so that we don't get carried away with debt and overwhelmed by anxiety. Many are afraid that a budget will hamper the freedom to spend money the way they want when they want. Some are afraid to look at the money situation; they might find out they don't have enough, so they don't look. But when you know exactly how much you make, what you spend, and what you have left over, you are free from the worry of not knowing. Sure, you might have to make changes in the way you spend, but the mystery is over. Budgets don't restrict you; they free you! Setting boundaries keeps you financially safe.

Relational

Your children and your former spouse may be your biggest challenges. Your guilt—whether genuine or false—can keep you locked in a dance that exhausts you.

Your kids may demand proof of your love for them

by insisting on getting their way, either passively or assertively. They may refuse to do their chores, complain about everything, only want to watch TV or play games, and pretty much ignore any family rules you try to impose. Even adult children will try to pull you into tugs of war. Your tendency may be to please them, to keep them "happy," or to avoid arguments in the home. After all, they have been so wounded by the divorce, how could you force them to clear their plates after dinner? Why, that would be like pouring salt into their wounds! Children need you to call them to a higher place—whether they feel like it or not. Remember that rules are for our safety, to help keep us all from falling off the cliff of selfishness and sin.

A whole book could be written about the layers of emotions, fears, guilt, and anxieties that linger between ex-spouses after a divorce and how to manage them. The goal is not to cut your former spouse out of your life—he or she will always be there—but to cut the negative emotional cords that still reach across town and keep you bound. Even if you get along well on the surface, try to see any harmful patterns of relating that might cause problems down the road.

And by the way, have you forgiven him or her? Perhaps more importantly, have you asked for forgiveness for all the ways *you* failed in the marriage? If not, do it soon.

Chapter 13

Build a Solid Roof

"DADDY, it's raining in Rosie's bedroom," little four-year-old Kaysie said rather tentatively. She stood there quietly to see if we'd come look.

My brother and his three little girls had come to visit, and he and I were sitting in the living room while the girls were scampering in and out of the other rooms in the house. A wet and windy desert storm was blustering outside.

"Yes, honey, it *is* rainy outside!" said my brother as we laughed. But I noticed a genuinely worried little look on Kaysie's face as her eyes grew wider. She insisted, this time a little louder.

"But Daddy, it IS raining in Rosie's bedroom."

She was distressed, and I sensed that feeling you get when you're trying to tell the whole world the sky is falling in and no one believes you! I got up, went into the bedroom, and saw that the whole sky was not falling—but the ceiling had. The roof had simply collapsed under the weight of the winter weather. There was a huge hole in the rafters, and Kaysie was right: it *was* raining in my bedroom!

The roof of the house—the life you are rebuilding—needs to be strong and secure. You'll want to make sure the basics are covered: finances, legal issues, support systems, and even stashing away a little something for a rainy day. But particularly after divorce, you will need a spiritual covering that will not cave in when life's storms rage on. Who and what will that be?

> For he will hide me in his shelter in the day of trouble; he will conceal me under the cover of his tent, he will set me high upon a rock.
>
> —Psalm 27:5

What is a spiritual covering?

In some church circles, the term *spiritual covering* has been misunderstood and misused. Some incorrectly claim it as a principle for being in strict authority over another to the point of controlling the other's life. That's not good.

> God alone is our secure "rooftop" covering, but He accomplishes that protection through others in our lives.

What *is* good is the truth that we are so deeply loved

that God Himself is our spiritual covering over all that would threaten to harm us. The Father, the Son, and the Holy Spirit give us refuge from the storms overhead. Here's what the Church teaches:

⋄ Jesus Christ is God—the Son, the Second Person of the Trinity.

⋄ Wherever the Son is, so always is the Father and the Holy Spirit. They are one.

⋄ We are one with Christ—albeit imperfectly until Heaven—through our baptism.

⋄ He is the Head, and through that baptism we are the members of His Body.

⋄ He desires to work through us to care for and tend to others.

So, yes, God alone is our spiritual covering because He desires that we be one with Him. He desires to work *through people* to bring His healing and help. God alone is our secure "rooftop" covering, but He accomplishes that protection through others in our lives.

Intercession is a protective covering

A father had nine children, and one son was always in trouble. When summer arrived and the family trip to Disneyland was approaching, the disobedient son was grounded and had to work a long list of chores to pay off the debt of money he owed his father. The children were so excited about going to the Magic Kingdom for the very first time that they couldn't stand the thought of their brother being left behind. In the days preceding the trip, one by one the children approached their father and begged him to give their brother reprieve. Some offered to do chores or hand over their allowance to pay off the brother's debt in time for the trip. The boy had done willful wrong, so the father remained stern and quiet, though he still listened lovingly to his children plead on their brother's behalf. The naughty son approached his father too and begged for mercy, offering to do extra penance and pay even more after the trip if only Dad would let him go.

Finally, the day before the trip, the father called all his children to him. "I'm so pleased with you all! You have showed love and sacrifice for your brother. He came to me himself to settle his debt, and my heart was moved for him. But how could I say no when I saw the love each of you had for him? I did not need you all to come to me, too, but I'm delighted that you did. You have given me great joy. Your brother is going to Disneyland!"

When we intercede for another, we offer our prayers as a covering, a protection, for that person. Clearly Jesus is first in line to plead (intercede) to the Father on behalf of us all. He's the first Mediator. On the Cross He paid the debt none of us could pay. Any time we pray to the Father, we do it through Christ in the power of the Holy Spirit. "Through Him, with Him, in Him [Jesus], in the unity of the Holy Spirit, all glory and honor is yours, Almighty Father, forever and ever. Amen."

The beauty of being in intimate union with Christ is that we become one with Him and then share in His life and His role as Intercessor. We can intercede for each other *through* Him.

The saints want to protect us too

Mary, our Mother, is not a dead Jewish woman who lived two thousand years ago or a plaster statue in the crying room at church. She's alive! In a sense, she and all the saints are more alive than they ever were on the earth. As our Mother, Mary constantly intercedes to her Son on our behalf and asks us to pray for one another as well. The rest of the saints in Heaven, who are filled with perfect love, also desire to intercede for us. And the saints still here on the earth— your friends, family, and those who pray for you—are able to intercede in their prayers for you and your intentions.

Prayer is a powerful covering. You need it. We all need it. Thanks to Jesus—our older brother and God's Firstborn, we can all go to our Father in Heaven and ask for favors. He delights in His children coming to Him on behalf of the rest of the family.

Covering some other basics

Good advice often attributed to St. Augustine—and reiterated by St. Ignatius of Loyola—says, "Pray as though everything depended on God; work as if everything depended on you." Once you have a spiritual covering in place, here are some other practical works that can keep you covered when the rains come.

Get a spiritual director

Start praying, looking around, and asking questions to find a spiritual director. This can be a priest or lay person, man or woman, but should be someone who is farther along in the spiritual journey than you so they can point you in the right direction. Are they completely faithful to the teachings of the Church? They'd better be.

Find a good babysitter

Too many single parents stay overwhelmed, overworked, and utterly drained because they do not make time for themselves to get away as Jesus did and have quiet or fun time in which to be renewed. Don't be a perpetual martyr; divorce is already a big enough cross. Instead, get a good babysitter. Can't afford one? Be creative: trade for housekeeping, ironing, reciprocal babysitting, or a lasagna casserole.

Get a good lawyer

Greedy grabbing for your possessions or finances is a way someone can tear your newly built life down to the ground. Scripture tells us to settle with our brother on the way to court if we can and to avoid legal wrestling. But sometimes it is absolutely necessary to protect the basics for you and your children. Don't be a martyr in this area, either, or try to save a buck by foregoing good legal counsel. You may have a responsibility to the children to wage a "just war" to get what they need.

Stash away a credit card

Make a plan to pay off all your debt as quickly as you are able, including cutting up every credit card you do not need. I said *need*, not *want*. Keep one card with a modest credit limit in a drawer and do *not* use it except in case of nuclear war! This will provide you with a financial covering.

Open a savings account

Even if you can get only one hundred dollars saved up in two years, it's something! A small financial covering can give a little bit of peace when the financial torrents hit.

Part 2

Make Your House a Home

It seemed like it took forever for the workers to cut down the trees, clear the lot, level it, and dig trenches for the plumbing and electric. The kids and I drove by every day, and it never looked like a house for months—we couldn't see anything happening. They put up a cyclone fence to keep people off the construction site, but we snuck in and walked around the framing. After the walls and roof went up, our realtor told us to start packing so we could move in! I couldn't wait to start throwing out all our old stuff. The dream was finally real!

—*Alan N., California*

Chapter 14

Clear Out Your Closets

"Lottery Winners Give It All Away"—I was fascinated by the *People* magazine article that showed an elderly man embracing his wife and placing a tender kiss on her forehead. Violet and Allen Large from Nova Scotia won $11.2 million and gave it to fourteen family members and sixty-three organizations, including their local fire station and hospital. What? Someone actually won the lottery and gave every penny away? "Money can't buy happiness," says Violet. "We have everything we need." They still drive their 1987 Dodge diplomat sedan.[1]

Sadly, very few of us have reached that level of detachment to material things, but that is where true freedom is to be found. How did your divorce leave you? Grasping tightly to the few things you still had? Fighting in court for years to get what you think is fair? You might relate more to the story of Bob, who learned the hard way that he always had everything he really needed.

Bob loses his stuff

After his wife filed for divorce, Bob moved out and rented an apartment. "I only had room for a small dinette with a few chairs, enough for me and the kids to have meals when they came to stay with me. I tried to make it a home, but it just wasn't. For the first few months, when they were not with me I would close the blinds, crawl up in a fetal position, and sink into depression. Many a night I fell asleep in my clothes curled up on a ball on my bed. It was hell."

Fast forward five years. Eventually Bob went through a lot of soul-searching and healing and received an annulment from the Church. He didn't think he'd marry again, but he found himself engaged and excited about a new life—doing it God's way this time. He found a little hillside home that would accommodate a new wife and his children. He gave notice to the landlady and began the laborious task of packing his things.

"That's when I went into another form of shock," Bob said. "I'd stockpiled so much stuff that every inch of every drawer was crammed. So I stopped packing, poured myself a beer, and went to watch TV. It was just too overwhelming."

Bob gets rid of his stuff

Bob had no idea what was to come next. As moving day drew nearer, he continually discovered that every room, every closet, and every drawer in his tiny place was filled with his things, much of which he'd owned since before he'd been married.

"My fiancée came to help, and she had a fit. *Why on earth do you have all this @#$%?* And she almost had a heart attack when she found out I had a separate storage room too. We were both physically exhausted from days of packing and lifting, and the thought of moving all those boxes into a new home was too much. We began to argue. She wanted me to throw everything out, and I just couldn't. I was overwhelmed—and attached."

Bob took some time to get honest about why he had so much old and unnecessary stuff and realized that *physical things had given him a sense of security and identity*. "I'd already suffered so many losses, including my marriage, my wife, my family, my home, my friends, and so much more. I couldn't also lose my things; they seemed to be all that was left of ME. After the divorce I realized it's like I reached my arms out wide, gathered as much as I could possibly hold, and hung on for dear life."

We can all be slaves to stuff

And that's the rebuilding tip for this chapter: detach from things. It's normal to hold on to possessions because of what they represent to us—our past, a person, a hope, or a dream. But they can weigh us down. The fear of being without things can enslave us. "Stuff" takes up space. It begs us to accumulate it, store it, and rent special trailers to carry it around with us. Even if it just sits there, it almost calls out softly to us every day, "Don't leave me! Keep me!

> It's normal to hold on to possessions because of what they represent to us—our past, a person, a hope, or a dream. But they can weigh us down.

The ideal time to jettison the junk is after a divorce and before you move into a new place. But that's not always possible or practical. Maybe you didn't have to move. Maybe you're the one who stayed in the house you shared before the divorce. Regardless, it's never too late to clean the cache!

We can all be slaves to relationships

It's not just "stuff" to which we get too attached; we can get far too focused on people—even those we love—and what we need or want from them.

> If any one comes to me and does not hate
> his own father and mother and wife and chil-
> dren and brothers and sisters, yes, and even his
> own life, he cannot be my disciple. Whoever
> does not bear his own cross and come after me,
> cannot be my disciple.
>
> —Luke 14:26–27

Hating your own children? Wait a minute. Unless we understand what Jesus was saying here, His words can sound harsh and even unloving. But we know Jesus is Love. He's warning us that we can idolize others— look at how we worship movie stars, sports stars, and music celebrities. Everyone wants a God, but not one who calls us to do hard things. So we make other people or things the god of our life—that which becomes most important to us. These false gods can be a beauti- ful source of comfort, security, peace, purpose, romance, affection, joy, and fun. But they will never last. They are not meant to be a here-and-now substitute for the eternal pleasures, comfort, and security of the one true God.

Let's take a look at how divorced people can stay stuck in a place of anxiety or unhappiness by making something or someone a false idol that we hope will make us happy.

Your former spouse

Have you convinced yourself that you will not be happy unless your ex comes back? While reconciliation is objectively a good thing, it's as if Jesus were saying, "I understand your sorrow, but you already have Me. Am I not enough for you?" We usually say, "Well, yes, Lord, but . . . "

Your children

"My kids are the center of my life!" Some parents (legally divorced or not) turn to their children for the sense of purpose, emotional affection, nurturing, or companionship they no longer get from a spouse. While they may have genuine affection for their child, a selfish element can also creep in, one that fears the loss of that child—or of his or her affection—to the degree that serenity, peace, and joy are also lost. "Smother mothers" are a good example of this. And there are smother fathers too.

A new romance

Is the desire of having someone to love driving you crazy? Have you convinced yourself you need someone? That it is not normal or healthy to be alone? Does it border on anxiety? Maybe you have convinced yourself you're just looking for another good parent for your child. Stop that! Being alone doesn't mean you have to be lonely. Although being without the comfort of another is definitely a cross to bear, no one ever *really* died of loneliness!

Jesus and our junk

God is not against things—He is the one who gave us the many gifts of creation and the ability to dream up and produce wonderful and useful inventions. We share in His creativity in that regard. So the problem is not with things—or our loving relationships—but with how attached we get to them. Do we lose our peace when we think we will not get what we want? Do we lack joy when we can't have what we think will make us happy or secure? Do we get fearful or angry because someone else has what we want?

In spiritual direction, this imbalanced need or craving is called an inordinate attachment, and it can be a disordered desire for a person, place, or thing. It's inordinate in that it becomes more important than God and the more-lasting spiritual gifts He has for us. Jesus dealt very clearly with this when He spoke with the rich young ruler who had run up, knelt before Him, and posed the question, "Good Teacher, what shall I do to inherit eternal life?" Do you remember what Jesus told him?

And Jesus said to him, "Why do you call me good? No one is good but God alone. You know the commandments: 'Do not commit adultery, Do not kill, Do not steal, Do not bear false witness, Honor your father and mother.'"

And he said, "All these I have observed from my youth."

And when Jesus heard it, he said to him, "One thing you still lack. Sell all that you have and distribute to the poor, and you will have treasure in heaven; and come, follow me."

But when he heard this he became sad, for he was very rich.

—Luke 18:18–23

The young man went away extremely disappointed. He did not want to give up the possessions to which he was so attached. They probably provided him with a strong sense of security, identity, comfort, and pleasure. Jesus was not condemning these things but calling the man to detach himself emotionally for greater things with more lasting value. It's as if Jesus said, "Hey, I can offer you much, much more. Will you trust Me?" (Jesus offers us much more too after the losses we experience in divorce.)

But the Bible story is not over; there's a hopeful ending. The apostles had been listening, and when the man walked away, Peter pointed out to Jesus that *they* had left everything to come follow Him. What would happen to them? Jesus made a beautiful promise to His disciples that He makes to us too:

> And he said to them, "Truly, I say to you, there is no man who has left house or wife or brothers or parents or children, for the sake of the kingdom of God, who will not receive manifold more in this time, and in the age to come eternal life."
>
> —Luke 18:29–30

That's the good news of the gospel. It's not just an ancient story—it's *our* story. Jesus invites everyone to a radical new way of life. When we detach from things, use and enjoy them wisely, and put the things of God first, we'll be on our way to eternal life.

What else did Jesus say about this? He reminded us that earthly things ultimately run out, run down, or rot.

> Do not lay up for yourselves treasures on earth, where moth and rust consume and where thieves break in and steal, but lay up for yourselves treasures in heaven, where neither moth nor rust consumes and where thieves do not break in and steal. For where your treasure is, there will your heart be also.
>
> —Matthew 6:19–21

Why some things just have to go

I came across a story that is a powerful visual about

the houses in which we live. Gunman Charles Carl Roberts IV entered the Nickel Mines Amish School in rural Lancaster County and shot to death five young girls and wounded others before killing himself. The story is tragic, but here's the nugget I want to develop: The school was subsequently torn down and the ground plowed under to do away with the visual reminder of the tragedy. A new schoolhouse, the New Hope Amish School, was built at a different location a few months later to serve the children in that district. No one could bear to even look at the old school, much less continue to use it. It was gone for good. Things in the visible world are often deeply connected to our experience with them, and when we see, hear, touch, or smell them, they have the power to take us through our memory or imagination to a place in our past that is either pleasant or not.

> After divorce there are things you may need to "tear to the ground and plow under," or at least throw in a bag and give to Goodwill.

After divorce there are things you may need to "tear to the ground and plow under," or at least throw in a bag and give to Goodwill. Even the smallest things can represent huge emotional issues, painful memories, or even fear. By all means get rid of them. If anyone suggests you are being too sensitive or immature, just smile and thank them for their concern. Here's a good time to practice those boundaries: don't explain, rationalize, or defend yourself. Change the subject. Keep that conversation out of your life.

Old Photographs

You have my permission to take down family or other photos that make you angry or stir up pain. But there is a right and wrong way to do this.

Don't:

◇ Deface or cut his or her face out and put the pictures back up on the mantle.

◇ Throw kerosene on them in the backyard and chant "Burn in Hell, you @#$!" Sadly, there are some recovery groups out there who encourage this kind of bitter, hateful action.

Do:

◇ Carefully pack them up and ask your ex *nicely* if he or she would like to have them.

◇ Set some or all aside in a special box for the children someday. If you can't stand seeing the box around, stick it up in the attic or storage area until you move. That's okay.

◇ Keep at least one picture of the other parent in the child's bedroom. It doesn't have to be huge. Always respect the permanent relationship your children have with their other parent.

Wedding Memorabilia

Do the same as above. Regardless of most circumstances, these will be particularly beautiful and poignant artifacts for your children when they become adults.

I kept our wedding album even though I wanted to burn it. My girlfriends wanted to have a divorce cocktail party and get rid of everything. They even showed me these divorce cakes you can order from the bakery. I wanted to, but I just couldn't do it. Even though we got an annulment and I understand that there was no sacramental marriage, there was a life together and our two kids. So I got one of those cardboard boxes from Staples that you put together yourself, and I packed it with the album, the cake knife I still had, and those engraved champagne flutes with our initials on them. When my children got married, I gave them each something from the box. They were so thankful.

—*Gerry*

His or Her Belongings

When you move or clean out closets you may find something that belonged to your former spouse. In fact, if you haven't done this yet, go through the house and garage and try to find such items and carefully clean and pack them. This practice can be an act of virtue.

I found my husband's golf shoes and some golf shirts from his favorite country club. I wanted to throw them in an old brown bag and shove them in his face next time I saw him. But it's like I heard God gently tap me on the shoulder and whisper, "Clean them." So I forced myself to wipe them down and clean out the dirt and grass that had stuck in the cleats, and I washed, ironed, and folded the shirts. Then I put them in a nice plastic bag. I can't believe I did it. While I was standing at the ironing board doing those shirts I cried. That act of kindness helped to get rid of some of the bitterness I'd been carrying around. Do I like him? No. Do I trust him? Probably never. But I can be kind, and that was the right thing to do.

—*Cherie*

When you still hang on to memories

There's an Internet urban legend showing a realistic

photo of a man who keeps his wife's dead body in a glass coffee table. Talk about hanging on to someone! That story might not be real, but this one is: a woman in Bradford County, Pennsylvania, dug up the graves of both her husband and twin sister after they died, brought their embalmed bodies home, put her husband in the garage (where I bet he used to like to putter!), and her sister in the guest bedroom. Police discovered the mummified bodies at the morbid scene after social workers visited the ninety-one-year-old woman at her home. Some people get so attached they can't let go.

Keeping a little something from your previous life after a divorce isn't bad, but if you find yourself refusing to part with something, you may still be overly attached and in need of letting go. I'm not talking about the normal furniture and kitchen pots that parting couples often take with them to survive (some people simply can't afford anything new) or small, sweet memorabilia that is tucked away somewhere. But if you find yourself still hanging on to something a little too much, ask God to help you complete the grieving process. Grief comes and goes, and we are never entirely rid of it. I still get teary-eyed if I think too long about my parents, who are both dead now. And even when writing about my former marriages, I can miss the parts that were good.

After divorce, some do a very good job of easily letting go of 99 percent—except that last little thing represents the totality of the loss. That totality can be the scary reality that the one remaining token helps them avoid. I always say, "When in doubt, throw it out." I know it's easier said than done; it may take some time. What is that one last thing you may possess that represents a life you once had, or still wish you did?

If you remarry

Some women can have a terrible emotional struggle with moving into a house you shared with *her*, using pots and pans *she* picked out fifteen years ago, and sleeping underneath a quilt that used to be on *your* bed together. This is real; don't minimize the feelings that can erupt over things in your new house that used to be part of your old life. You could be right that the upset person needs to "get over it." But that is between them and God, and they need your support to get to that place.

I was so excited to marry Brad and start our life together. He had a huge California king sized bed he'd recently bought for us, and we'd received gorgeous Egyptian cotton sheets for a wedding present. He didn't really have anything of his ex-wife's that I could see, and he'd told me that he pretty much had to buy all new household items when he moved out after the divorce. We'd combined a lot of our things for the new home, including a soft cotton quilt he had which was now on our bed. One night I commented on how beautiful it was—I really did like it a lot—and asked where he'd purchased it. "Oh, I don't remember," he said casually, "Barbara picked it out I think." "Barbara? You mean it was on your old bed with her?" I jumped out of bed and told him as calmly as I could that I wanted to change the blanket because I just could not sleep under that quilt.

He got upset and said I was being irrational and told me to get back into bed. I refused because I wanted him to listen. To understand. Couldn't we just get a new blanket? We got into a big argument, and I started crying. It escalated, and he said he couldn't believe this was all over a stupid quilt. But it wasn't the quilt—it's what it represented to me.

She was still always sticking her nose into our private business. They had kids together, and we didn't yet. I was still struggling with some insecurity because I know that even an attempted marriage creates a powerful bond. Heck, even just plain sex creates a bond. I didn't want memories of her in our home.

I slept on the sofa. In the morning we talked. I was calmer, and he really listened. "Honey, I get it. We can get a new quilt." When he said that, I hugged him and I was fine. I realized as long as he was willing to get a new quilt and throw that one out, I was okay with keeping it. So we did. But I washed it in really hot water and threw some Clorox in there too. Ha ha ha. It just made me feel better.

—*Anonymous*

As I heard this story I realized that even the washing and adding of Clorox by this woman was an outward use of physical objects—visible, tangible matter—to represent inner emotional realities. In this case, a fresh new start and making sure none of the old is left. Sometimes matter does matter.

Packing tips

◇ Decide you're not going to be overly attached to things any more. Your emotions might fight you, but remember your intellect is in charge!

◇ Ask God for the grace to start placing your security—and identity—in Him.

◇ Decide to give your house a complete thinning out, no matter what or how long it takes. Give yourself six months or a year to do it or you may be overwhelmed and quit after cleaning out the trunk of your car!

◇ Get a calendar. Make a list of all the areas in your home (or storage facility) that need to be cleaned out and number them. Then write all the areas that need thinning down one week at a time on the calendar. Every week just take care of one small area. Soon it will be finished.

◇ Start with the kitchen junk drawer. Then the pots and pans. Do you really need five spatulas?

◇ Every time you go through one of your areas, set aside three boxes or big bags for KEEP, TRASH, and DONATE. Then arrange your stuff accordingly. When you're finished, go back through that KEEP box and get tough; move more into the DONATE or TRASH boxes. Then do it again.

◇ Call the thrift store right away to come get your donations, or pack it up and take it down to your church.

◇ Get your kids a calendar and have them do this with their rooms.

◇ When you just can't let go of something you know isn't necessary or is taking up too much time or energy, ask God to reveal what the fear is behind your attachment. He's just waiting to give you the grace to let go.

Chapter 15

Stock Up Your Kitchen

"PLEASE sir, may I have some more?" Do you recall the smudged but cherubic face of the little waif Oliver in the movie musical of the same name? He stood in the dark and dingy orphanage with hundreds of other thin, tattered, and starving orphans—with arms outstretched, holding high their empty wooden bowls, plaintively singing "Food, glorious food!" and begging for some small scraps from the cruel headmaster. They were starving.

After divorce, when we've lost all that seemed to emotionally fill us up, we can also be starving in a lot of other ways.

Our disordered appetites

Did you ever wonder why the story of Adam and Eve points to the forbidden as a juicy piece of fruit? That succulent temptation, and all the power of self-determination Adam and Eve perceived it would bring them, was something they desired more than they desired to love God. God should have been first; instead they put Him second. That appetite was out of order. As a result of their sin, we too have what the Church calls disordered appetites. We feed on other delights; God no longer comes first.

Food—and the way we relate to it—is an-easy-to-understand sign of deeper spiritual mysteries. The Church teaches that we have good and natural appetites for security, companionship, belonging, comfort, nurturing, pleasure, sex, and love. We hunger for these things because God made us to desire them. He wants us to view them rightly as gifts that ultimately point us to Him, who is the perfect and endless source of each of them. They satisfy for a while; He satisfies forever.

But when we look past God, like Adam and Eve did, and our desires are disordered to greediness, selfishness, and using others, they become sinful and eventually bring about some sort of death. After divorce, when these earthly joys have been taken from us, how do we feed ourselves in a healthy way? And where do we go to stop the hunger pangs?

Poverty of spirit, starving for love

Mother Teresa of Calcutta worked for years with the starving people in India. But she often expressed pity for the "poverty-stricken West." She would tell those who interviewed her that spiritual and emotional poverty of the Western world is much greater than the physical poverty of India. After my divorce, I knew exactly what she meant when she talked about those who were "poor in spirit and starving for love." The stomach and the heart can be similar. People everywhere are not hungry in the physical sense, but they are in another way. What they are missing is an intimate, living relationship with God.

Fast-food nation

Christopher West and I were talking together about the illicit and foolish places where people go to feed their hungers for love. He told me:

> In some of my older talks, I'd used to use the analogy of people eating out of a dumpster instead of the lavish banquet that God has prepared for us. Analogies are never perfect, but the dumpster image still didn't quite ring true. I realized that dumpsters stink, and rotten food tastes bad. The unlawful things people pursue to feed their appetites do look, smell, and truly taste delicious! For a while. The heart attack or life-threatening disease that comes later, even decades later, is not that apparent or we wouldn't "eat" there. Now when someone looks for love

in all the wrong places, I compare it to eating fast food. Those Mickey D fries taste good right now, but the harmful physical effects of a steady diet of high-fat, high-sugar, and high-sodium fast food may not show up for years.

Are you a fast-food junkie when it comes to feeding your appetites for security, companionship, love, and intimacy? St. John of the Cross was a Spanish mystic who wrote

> ⬦
>
> Are you a fast-food junkie when it comes to feeding your appetites for security, companionship, love, and intimacy?
>
> ⬦

about our appetites standing in the way of our union with God. The major points in *The Ascent of Mount Carmel* (book 1, chapters 6–9) are ones to which most of us can relate:

> Inordinate appetites weary a soul because they can never be satisfied. This causes a person to feel restless, discontent, fatigued, burdened, oppressed, disturbed, and upset.
>
> Disordered attachments to creatures torment a soul because they enslave the will and limit its freedom. This causes a person to feel afflicted, wounded and hurt, anguished, and weighed down by cares and desires.

Disordered affectivity darkens the soul because it reduces the clarity of the intellect, causing the person to experience weakness of the will and dullness of the memory.

Disordered appetites defile a soul because they diminish the person as an image of God.

Food, glorious food

The song in the musical *Oliver!* has special meaning for Catholics—our God comes to us as food, glorious food! The Eucharist is indeed "the living bread which came down from heaven,"[1] as Jesus described Himself.

The other night I shared the most wonderful meal with someone very special: a large loaf of fresh-baked and still-warm French bread, with sweet butter, and two flutes of chilled, sparkling champagne. That was it—just bread and wine! I know we didn't cover all the food groups, but it was Heaven. After our meal, we were stuffed and, perhaps more accurately, satisfied and intoxicated. Believe it or not, this points to something mysterious and even delicious about God.

It's no mystery that Jesus comes to us as food and drink, since without it we die. Without Him, we also die. Food and drink are the very first things that a human baby desires, and I believe that experience begins to point the way to the fulfillment of that first desire—the Eucharistic Jesus. And Jesus comes to us not just as any food but as bread and wine.

Bread is the universal food that stops the hunger pangs and is delicious.

Wine gives us a sense of calm and well being and is intoxicating.

Did you know that the Catholic Church will not use mere grape juice to consecrate into the blood of Jesus at the Mass? It must be the juice of crushed grapes, as Jesus was crushed out of love for us. It must have been changed in the fermenting process to produce a feeling of euphoria, as the soul should feel when in union with God. Wine has long been a sign in the Gospels of God's intoxicating love. Jesus performed His first miracle at the wedding feast of Cana when the young couple (symbolizing us all) had run out of wine (symbolizing God's love). Jesus came to overflow our jars with God's love—a holy inebriation!

> Wisdom has built her house, she has set up her seven pillars. She has slaughtered her beasts, she has mixed her wine, she has also set her table. She has sent out her maids to call from the highest places in the town, "Whoever is simple, let him turn in here!" To him who is without sense she says, "Come, eat of my bread and drink of the wine I have mixed."
>
> —Proverbs 9:1–5

We can crave other things, but Jesus is the food and drink that truly satisfies.

They say you are what you eat. After a divorce you're going to be filling the larder of your new life with some kind of food that you think will fill you up. What's it going to be? Are you hungry for possessions, power, money, or revenge? Are you starving for new love? Is what you seek to fill the gnawing in your heart truly satisfying? Does it intoxicate you with love for God?

Chapter 16

Make Your Bedroom Special

"Knock-knock!"
"Who's there?"
"Jesus."
"Uh, do you mean, like, Jesus the Son of God?"
"Yes. May I please come in?"
Uh-oh, better pick up the place.
"Okay! Just a minute!"

I'LL bet you know what it's like to make a mad dash around the house to pick up the mess before company comes in. You might be able to make the living room presentable, but with those back rooms—especially the bedroom—you'll just have to lock the door and keep the company from going down the hall.

I've heard more than one Christian chastity speaker compare a person's life to a house full of rooms where no one wants Jesus going down the hall and into their bedroom. Christ can sit down in the living room for a lemonade and stay with us for supper in the dining room, but the bedroom is off limits. That's because there are things that go on there that we *know* would not please Him.

For a long time I struggled with the Church's teachings on sex and decided I knew better than that outdated morality. I was a modern woman, and the Church simply needed to get with the times. What did those old pinched-face church ladies know about passion anyway? I wanted Jesus—and all the blessings and grace I knew He could give me—but I didn't want anyone telling me what to do with my body. I became a "cafeteria Catholic," picking and choosing what I believed and obeyed, or didn't. Although I experienced temporary fun and excitement, the poison of sin was slowly killing me. But I didn't care. I didn't want to endure the pain of loneliness, especially after divorce.

Loneliness makes us hungry for love

When I asked divorced men and women to tell me how they handled the loneliness after divorce, these are some of the answers I received:

I was okay. I had been single for seventeen years prior to the divorce, so I am sure I had a big advantage on everyone. I just went back to working, enjoying my friends, and living my life.

—*Patricia*

I dated a woman for about a year and a half but have not been actively dating since we broke up a couple of years ago. I find that I'm not really that motivated to date anyone right now. I think I need more time to heal.

—*J.C.*

I absolutely hate dating. I always said, "I'll go to lunch or dinner or a show with you, but we're not calling it a date!" In my experience men read wa-a-a-y too much into things, and, for me, we're gonna develop a friendship and then consider more—or it just ain't gonna happen!

—*Marsha*

These following responses, all from women, show a fear that comes from not knowing how to approach the whole subject of new relationships.

I am scared, very, very scared. It's just easier for me not to date. Then I don't have any "situations" to deal with. —*Patty*

I feel too dirty and disgusted with myself to lower myself and settle for someone who doesn't cherish me. So no physical intimacy.

—*Marsha*

I don't date. Not going there.

—*Anonymous*

My friend Daniel DiSilva is funny and smart, an accomplished Catholic artist and musician—and divorced. He shared some insights about the emotional pain men feel after divorce or any deep injury to the heart:

> Sometimes men's hearts break harder than women's, and that's why we don't talk about it— it's just too painful. While many women tend to wear their hearts on their sleeves—and can easily express their sorrow—we men have to keep our sleeves rolled up to be the strong ones. We've been conditioned to be cold and calloused on the surface, but that's often to protect the tender part inside.

> Sometimes men's hearts break harder than women's, and that's why we don't talk about it—it's just too painful.

> You know that popular image of the man with three nails in his hand and Christ is holding him up as he sags in sorrow to his feet? That is the posture that all men ultimately long to be in—collapsed in the strong and loving arms of Christ. But we can't yet—not until the end. We have to stay strong for the rest of the world. It's hard. It hurts. But we know we have to be that

strong Christ for others. And some people just don't understand that.

Jesus is the Bridegroom and we are the Bride

In chapter 11 (about annulments) you read about Jesus as the Bridegroom and us as the Bride, which is part of what the Church calls the spousal analogy in Scripture. God has always used pictures and parables for us to begin to understand Him and His love for us. These images reveal something of God's innermost self. You know some of the other analogies in Scripture:

Like a shepherd, He tends to us and leads us safely through life.

Like a grape vine, He bears fruit through us, His branches.

Like a father, He waits for us to return home to eat the fatted calf.

But the most profound biblical image of His eternal love for us is the image of a bride and groom, with Heaven described as the eternal wedding feast. It's romantic, powerful, and passionate.

In the Old Testament God revealed Himself through the prophets to be like a husband, and His people like unfaithful wives. In the New Testament, Jesus proclaims Himself the Bridegroom, and Heaven is described as the eternal wedding feast.

This spousal analogy reveals that love, marriage, and sex are not something apart from God—although we have tried desperately to separate them—but all are rooted in the deep and tender love God has for us. Love that calls us into a permanent, life-giving marriage with Him. It's not a perfect analogy and is mystical in nature, but look at it this way:

◇ God desires intimate communion with us forever.

◇ He passionately pursues our hearts as a bridegroom pursues his bride.

◇ He reveals His love and promises so that we will open up our hearts to Him.

◇ When we open to receive Him into our lives, He draws close to make us one with Him.

◇ He fills us with the "seed" of a share in His divine life.

◇ His divine life and love grow in us, and we "deliver" them out into the world.

In this image all of us—men included—share in some way in being a beautiful bride. But don't worry! Men will not have to cease being men to enter into this mysterious picture of how the heart should be completely trusting, open, and receptive to God. Like a man resisting a bridal imagery, we women might not feel very comfortable with other images in Scripture—like

St. Paul's masculine military analogy of a soldier preparing for battle—but they illustrate profound truths that apply to everyone.

> Put on the whole armor of God, that you may be able to stand against the wiles of the devil's tactics. . . . Stand therefore, having girded your loins with truth, and having put on the breastplate of righteousness, and having shod your feet with the equipment of the gospel of peace; besides all these, taking the shield of faith, with which you can quench all the flaming darts of the evil one. And take the helmet of salvation, and the sword of the Spirit, which is the word of God.
>
> —Ephesians 6:11, 14–17

The devil wants to destroy the sign

In the spousal analogy it's pretty obvious that—in a certain spiritual sense—God wants to make us one with Him, "marry" us, and "impregnate" us with divine life and love. That is the meaning of life and why we exist: sweet, loving union with God. When the human soul says "I do" to Him, we can live forever with Him.

Marriage between a husband and wife is the sign that points us to that kind of love. If we can love each other as God loves us, then we find the path to Heaven—literally! Now, imagine that a neon sign flashed "Heaven this way" and had a big gold button that read "push here." When you pushed the button you'd immediately get swept off your feet and carried in a cloud up to the Pearly Gates. That is what the Sacrament of Marriage does. Not only is it a sign, but when we live it the right way, it has the power to transport us up into this Heavenly exchange of love between Christ and His Bride. Caught up in their embrace, we can drink deeply from the life that flows between them.

The way that Jesus loves His Bride, the Church (which is all of us), is the road map for a marriage that takes us to Heaven.

Jesus' love is free, so the enemy wants us to be fearful, pressured, and enslaved. Christ has no fears, pressure, or anxiety about being one with ("marrying") us. He could say no, but He freely desires us and freely gives Himself to us.

Jesus' love is full, so the enemy wants us to withhold from each other. Jesus holds nothing back. He gives all of Himself to us, for the fullness of time, even His life by dying on a cross to save us from Hell.

Jesus' love is faithful, so the enemy wants us to use each other. Jesus would never say or do a thing that might bring us harm of any kind. Everything He says or does is meant to bring us the greatest good we could ever have: Heaven.

Jesus' love is fruitful, so the enemy wants us to practice contraception. When you have God's love, you have His divine life. Where there is love, there must be life. God Himself *is* Life and Love, and you cannot separate the two. In that spiritual embrace with God, we open our hearts to be filled with His life.

The only relationship that can mirror love that is free, full, faithful, and fruitful is marriage between a man and woman that is permanent, exclusive, and open to life. Every other type of "love" not only falls short but will ultimately collapse in pain and suffering—even death. Jesus shows us the right way—and, in fact, He *is* "the Way."

Redefining marriage

Satan does not want us getting anywhere near Heaven. He hates us and wants us dead. He doesn't have the power to kill us, but he can turn the "sign" of marriage around—as it were—to point the other way so we go the wrong direction and drive right off a cliff! Over the last few decades the enemy has succeeded in getting many of us to believe the big lie about love, marriage, and sex—just like he did with Eve!

"Can you really trust God? He's trying to withhold something you deserve! You should be free to eat *any* fruit you want, including that one He said 'Don't touch.' You *know* you want it!"

Now change *God* to *the Church*:

"Can you really trust the Church? She's trying to

withhold something you deserve! You should be free to have sex *any* way or time you want, including the ones She said 'Don't do.' You *know* you want it!"

It made sense to Eve, but she ended up homeless, suffering, and facing death. It makes sense to us, but we will end up homeless, suffering, and facing death of possibly more than one kind when we ignore Christ and His Bride, the Church.

Hiding in the Jesus-is-my-husband analogy

Everything that is good, true, and beautiful can be twisted into something unhealthy, including the spousal analogy. Men can squirm in their seats if they think this is a sexual image. It's not. It's a heavenly image that should help us all understand the nature of the soul being intimately open to receive God. But women can get this analogy wrong too. I've met too many women—married and divorced—who use the marital image of Jesus as their "husband" as a hiding place to avoid the hard work of real love. Let me give you an example:

Melinda felt trapped in her marriage. She and her husband, Gerry, had hit a wall, and nothing seemed to be working. She didn't want to divorce—too much shame and too scary financially—so she decided to find refuge in Jesus. In itself, running to Him is not a bad thing, but it should be done in the right spirit. Melinda began going to prayer meetings, went to Mass more frequently, and started a small women's Bible study in her home. She and her husband lived like roommates in the same house while he retreated into work and television and she into her romance with Jesus. After all, Jesus was perfect, loving, kind, strong, and faithful to the end. He was the perfect husband—Gerry wasn't. Melinda kindly tolerated Gerry, who also resigned himself to no more work on their marriage. It was easier for both of them with her "new" husband. Even though there were a lot of new pictures of Jesus around, there was no love in their house.

This is a way people can love God but "use" Him at the same time. Jesus said that if we want to love Him, we have to love others. What we do to and for others, we do to and for Him. Melinda was tired of the struggles in her marriage and didn't want to endure the frustration of Gerry's humanity. She considered having to stay with Gerry, a suffering that she offered up to God, while refusing the greater suffering that came with *really* trying to love Gerry. She could have gone to marriage counseling, tried something new, or perhaps changed her own selfish ways. Those are hard. Ignoring her husband and constantly comparing him to Jesus was easier, but it wasn't love.

I've also heard from men who had to live in relationships like this, and they admit they gave up in their marriages, saying, "He's God. I'm not. I could never compare to Him."

Sherry's case is similar. She was hurt and bitter over

her divorce and annulment, turned to Christ, and found great comfort in His love. Her prayer life deepened, and she began to hunger for more of God. But she was still carrying unhealed wounds toward men, some going back to her own divorced father, and she refused to date. She was afraid of ever being hurt again and was reluctant to learn relationship skills or come out of her comfort zone. When Sherry shared with people at her church that Jesus was her husband, they all nodded at how spiritual she was. After divorce some women make a choice for lifelong singlehood for a variety of good, healthy, and holy reasons. Others do not; they're still enslaved to hurt or fear. Every case is different, and each involves many complex layers of the human heart and soul.

Is Jesus your husband? He is—in a mystical sense— and that means He wants the hearts of all men and women open and receptive so that He can be in a loving, permanent, and life-giving union with us. But never at the expense of running or hiding from the demands of authentic love right here on earth.

Love and marriage are very difficult; no one knows that like a divorced person. That's why we need to have all of God's graces possible to help us be able to love freely, fully, faithfully, and fruitfully. To love like Christ will always mean having to carry one's own cross and be crucified on it for the greater good of the other.

That's where true joy is. That's the *true love* you've always desired.

Chapter 17

Keep Up on Your Cleaning

LAST week it rained for five days and nights in a row. Even inside my house, I had to wear two sweaters and sip on hot tea to keep the chill away.

But today I am wearing a short-sleeved T-shirt and sitting barefoot at my computer. I have a glass of ice-cold Crystal Light, all the windows are wide open, and a warm, fragrant breeze is blowing through the house. It's spring!

I have to finish this book, but do you know what I *really* want to do? Open up all the closets and clean them out. Go down to Bed, Bath & Beyond and buy shelving to get everything better organized. Call the neighborhood charity truck to come haul away the junk I need to throw out. Boy, would I feel great after that.

Spring cleaning of the soul

Spring is the time that you can open up the windows and let the fresh air blow away the musty smells and the winter cobwebs. Our soul needs spring cleaning too. In our house analogy for your life after divorce, closets represent the areas where you may have shoved a lot of stuff you do not want to get rid of but you don't want anyone to see. In the springtime after the dark winter of a divorce, the Holy Spirit can come into the dank, moldy closets of our lives and make them fresh again. He specializes in getting rid of junk, trash, spiders, rats, and even mushroom-like fungi that sprout out of the floor carpet.

> In the springtime after the dark winter of a divorce, the Holy Spirit can come into the dank, moldy closets of our lives and make them fresh again.

Bob told me his closet story.

I'd stored some of my tennis racquets in the very back of my big bedroom closet. They'd been there for years, behind piles of old shoes and clothes I'd been saving and never donated, and who-knows-what else in there. One day I decided to move it all out and try to find those tennis racquets. I was pretty disgusted with myself after bringing out boxes and boxes of all the ridiculous stuff I'd been saving, but I got an even bigger surprise when I found the racquets.

Apparently the adjacent bathroom tub/shower combination had been leaking for years under the floor. The shag carpet at the back of the closest was a huge colony of brown trumpet mushrooms that had grown up about three inches high and into and through the strings of all my racquets. Some of the clothes were ruined too, and I had to wash them all even to get them ready to give to Goodwill. It was nasty.

Yep, nasty. That's exactly what you could call the dark, hidden sins that can rot away the beautiful lives we are trying to build after divorce. In this chapter I want to help you open up the closet doors of your life and take stock of what's in there. When I work with divorced men and women, I've found that some of the nasty stuff is the same for many people, so let's see if any of them are something you need to throw out or wash.

Unforgiveness

In my popular DVD series, *The Catholic's Divorce Survival Guide*, I cover the wide range of emotions with which people struggle, like anger, guilt, grief, fear, depression, and loneliness. But I save the topic of forgiveness for last because that is often the hardest with which to deal. Refusing to forgive is a hardness of heart that can kill. It keeps the moldy mushrooms of anger and bitterness alive, and those will destroy the grace in the soul. God's love and divine life in our hearts cannot live when they are smothered by a colony of spiritual fungi.

Why is forgiveness often so difficult? Because:

◇ *You are afraid for it to be completely over.* When you forgive someone, you know it's over and you have to let go of it all. Maybe you don't feel ready, and the ability and willingness to completely let go after divorce is taking a long time. Part of you still needs or wants to be connected—even in a negative way.

◇ *You like the feeling of control.* When you refuse to give someone something that they may not deserve and will bless them, you can retain a sense of control over the situation. After all, they took so much away from you! But now you're playing God.

◇ *You are afraid that they will get away with the injustice.* It doesn't seem fair to give someone the gift of forgiveness when they have no intention of acknowledging their offenses against you or of repenting. In fact they may be gleefully continuing to try to harm you. That's just not right—right?

⬦ *You don't trust God.* You don't trust that God
   will do what He has always promised: bring
   sins to light, expose the sinner, and bring
   about perfect justice. That would make you
   feel good. You don't want to wait until the
   last judgment—you want justice now! I
   know that feeling. God will do all that He
   has promised, but on *His* timetable and in
   His way, not yours. He'll also have great
   mercy and maybe let them off with a light
   sentence or none at all. Stop and think
   about how wonderful that is because someday you may need that same mercy—and
   even much more of it!

Decide today that you will forgive the other person, be it an ex-spouse, the judge, an attorney, an in-
law, a friend, a family member, or someone else who has
wronged you in the divorce. *Forgiveness is an act of the
will, not a feeling.* Even when you don't feel like it, do
it. Trust God and let go. And remember, you may have
to keep forgiving these people many times for future
offenses. If you don't forgive, you make it impossible
for God to forgive you. How do we know that? Look at
how Jesus taught us to pray. "Forgive us our sins as we
forgive others" means just that. As we do it to others,
God will do it to us. Or not.

Do you have to like the person if you forgive them? No. Jesus forgave those who crucified Him even as He was hanging on the Cross. I am pretty sure He loved them (wanting the salvation of their souls) and forgave them, but I imagine He wasn't very happy with the choices they'd made. He was fully human, not a robot.

Do you have to trust them if you forgive them? No. Trust can be violated and must be earned. That takes time, and it takes two. Trust may be lost forever. Trust God instead.

Do you have to pretend what they did was not wrong or hurtful? No. Forgiveness doesn't mean you check your brains at the door. Acknowledge it, but stop thinking and talking about it all the time.

Do you have to forget all about it? Not always. Sometimes it's good to remember how someone can hurt you so you can stay safe in the future.

Do you even have to talk to them again if they are still hurting you? No. Don't be vengeful and always remain kind, but don't try to be friends if the person truly is not a friend to you. Forgiveness means:

◇ You give them to God and ask Him to give you the same mercy

◇ You release your desire for justice to God's way of doing it

◇ You free yourself to receive God's graces

Bitterness

Let's say you may have made the decision in your will to forgive someone—perhaps your ex-spouse—but you admit you still feel bitter. How does that happen? After the act of your will in forgiving them, your focus may shift from their offenses to your life, and that's when the sour taste in your mouth still remains. Look how terrible life is! It was unfair! Look how much you lost! Look at how poor, lonely, stressed, or afraid you are! Look at how hard you have to work . . . and on and on and on. You may have forgiven in your head but not in your emotions. You are bitter.

> Like a fungus that eventually takes over and kills its host, the bitterness we harbor as a result of our divorces can invade and destroy our emotional, physical, and spiritual health.

Jeff admitted to a great deal of anger in his divorce. He made the move to forgive, but he still struggled with bitterness:

> I was still very emotionally attached to money and financial success. . . . With the divorce, I got saddled with huge debt since my

ex-wife never worked. So I was responsible for paying all of the debts, alimony, child support, plus an enormous amount of fictitious equity in our San Diego house. I say fictitious equity because the house ultimately sold for $400,000 less than it was appraised at as a result of the downturn in the economy. I still had to pay her the full equity that was only on paper when the house was worth nearly $900,000. I never received any equity from the house. All I got was debt. In fact, here it is nearly six years after our divorce and I am still paying off doctor bills as well as our contractor. I truly have made the decision to forgive her, but all of this has left me with a bad taste in my mouth.

I have another disgusting fungus story, from the section on bitterness in my book *Healing the Divorced Heart*,[1] a devotional with short meditations on the emotions you may feel after a divorce:

Sweet-smelling grasses and pungent pine trees grow thick and green in the breathtakingly beautiful lakeside forests of Michigan's Upper Peninsula. No one would suspect that lurking just below the surface of this postcard-pretty picture is the giant, life-sucking Armillaria bulbosa fungus, one of the world's largest living organisms. The fifteen-hundred-year-old fungus covers over thirty-seven acres (more than five football fields), weighs in excess of a hundred tons (the weight of about fifty cars), and is described by botanists as "roughly the texture of rotting fabric." Most of the fungus lives underground, but tree-rot and mushroom growth are visible signs on the surface.

Bitterness hides much the same way in our lives. We may be professionally coifed, manicured, and fit, with perfect church attendance and beautiful clothes with shoes to match! We might be fierce prayer warriors, hard workers, wonderful mothers, friends, or selfless volunteers . . . but just beneath the surface hides the rotting root of bitterness. Bitterness can take the form of anger, self-pity, general irritability, anxiety, or feelings of hopelessness.

Like a fungus that eventually takes over and kills its host, the bitterness we harbor as a result of our divorces can invade and destroy our emotional, physical, and spiritual health. Our problems that we might think are isolated or unrelated to our divorces can actually be symptoms of a giant root of bitterness. Are you harboring resentments beneath your surface? They're keeping you from being the most beautiful and healthy creation God intended.

Chapter 18

Don't Hide Things in the Cellar

SOME homes have cellars—the creepy place in horror movies where they sometimes bury the bodies or where the boogie man is always waiting!

The cellar of your life may be the part that's deep down below the surface where all kinds of things may hide in the dark, worse than what is in the upstairs closet. If you're rebuilding a new life after divorce, you'll want to make sure that you don't bring, or store in the cellar, any secret—or not-so-secret—addictions.

Dealing with addictions

Addictions are the disordered (sinful) ways we self-medicate when we don't have the wisdom or courage to deal with pain and sufferings. I'm not talking about watching TV, spending, eating, or drinking a little too much now and then. God has been merciful to give us beautiful things of the world to calm and soothe us. I'm talking about those things we know are wrong and with which we struggle to overcome; things that have negative effects in your life before, during, and after a divorce.

Your struggle may or may not be sinful, but get some help from a good spiritual director. Pray about it, and get others to pray for you as well. You do not want to bring these into a new life, whether it is as a single person or with a new spouse. They fall into these major categories:

> Addictions are the disordered (sinful) ways we self-medicate when we don't have the wisdom or courage to deal with pain and sufferings.

Overeating

Food is comforting, but it can be a substitute for the comfort God wants us to find in Him and can hide a lack of skills in dealing with the reality of life. It also can be a severe threat to your health.

Overdrinking

Scientists have recently proven what Scripture has always told us: a little wine is good for us! "No longer drink only water, but use a little wine for the sake of your stomach and your frequent ailments." —1 Timothy 5:23

But too much alcohol, or drinking for the wrong reasons, signals a spot in our cellar that needs cleaning. Even if you have "just one glass at dinner each night," see if you can stop for a week.

Overspending

You can be addicted to online shopping, catalogs, the mall where you addictively consume clothes, shoes, cars, jewelry, and more. Gambling and even spending too much money on lottery tickets can all signal areas where you need to get some balance or professional help.

Overactivity

Workaholism is a disorder too. So is losing yourself on the Internet, video games, Xbox, or other electronic distractions that put you into a state of detachment and disinterest in other people. In counseling sessions during Catholic marriage preparation weekends for young couples, I hear the same complaint in every group: the guys spend too much time watching TV, surfing the Internet, and playing video games. The young women are fearful they are marrying little boys, and they may be right. The preoccupation with games and an inability to turn them off could be early signs of a future divorce.

Overemphasis on appearance

This is a growing addiction—or at least a disordered priority—in a culture that has sold us the lie that a beautiful (and youthful) body will get us all the love and sex we want. Because of that inordinate desire, you can be addicted to exercising, running, or going to the gym, or you could be constantly improving your hair, skin, and makeup regimen. It's all based on fear.

Pornography and Masturbation

This is the one no one wants to talk about, but it kills your ability to truly love. The culture lies about it, telling us that it's necessary for healthy, normal sexual behavior and that everyone is doing it. These actions train you to see people as things and reduce them to objects to be used for your self-focused pleasure. That is not healthy, normal, or loving.

Christopher West borrows from Pope John Paul II's writings when he says, "We could say that the problem with pornography is not that it reveals too much of the person, but that it reveals too little. Indeed, it portrays the naked human body without revealing the person at all."[1]

In other words, pornography is not interested in the men and women it portrays; it is only interested in reducing them to body parts to be sold and used by consumers, not unlike a mad scientist conducting amputations on live people and passing around their limbs for someone else's pleasure. Because of the high level of stimulus and chemicals involved, pornography can be as addictive as crack cocaine, and today it is the number one addiction in our country. It's also a major symptomatic problem in a high number of marriages. Spouses who should be sexually available, in love, to each other are having to compete with something much faster, much easier, and sometimes more exciting. The "other woman" doesn't live on the other side of town anymore; she's on the computer or in a stack of magazines under the bed.

Men are not the only ones who keep this secret hidden in their cellars. In an effort to normalize this addictive sin and cast off the healthy shame that comes with it, even women's magazines—and some current TV shows and movies—continue to promote pornography and masturbation as healthy and normal. I remember a woman in one of my divorce recovery groups who cried when I shared with the class that masturbation was a sin because it misused the gift of our sexuality and trained our minds and bodies to be selfish.

She told me, "I knew the Church said it was wrong but I never understood why. So I just ignored it. No one ever explained it to me like that." She told me that her girlfriends—all high-income, professional women— had given her a divorce party and sex toys as presents. I asked her if she'd be willing to throw them away and begin a new life. She burst into tears again. "I'm not sure

I can. I'm all alone; it's all I have left," she said, sobbing.

The danger of pornography or even intense romance novels for women is not only the physical addiction but the emotional attachment. After all, God made a wife to freely and fully attach all of herself to the husband she loves. And now women are attaching themselves to inanimate objects. We are so confused and wounded. Sweet Lord, have mercy on us.

Over concern about animals

Another possible addiction that (mostly) woman can develop is over-attachment to their pets. How many magazine articles have you read that said single (or divorced) women should get themselves a cat or a dog to keep them company? Sure, pets are a gift God has given us for nurturing, pleasure, and companion-ship. But just as food, drink, and other gifts can become the center of our universe, so can pets. Here's an example: many divorced Catholic women who are free to date have joined Catholic singles groups. What do they want in a spouse? The most common description I hear is they want a new mate who has a good income, can dance, and is a faithful Catholic man. I used to run a large Catholic singles group in my diocese in Southern California, and I would have a conversation like this every few months:

"Audrey! How is that romance with Pat going?"

"Oh, that's over."

"What? He was so nice. So perfect for you. Retired, good income, and you two looked great on the dance floor last month. And he's a faithful Catholic. What happened?"

"Well, he's allergic to Fritzi."

"Your cat? Are you kidding me? Audrey, this guy was in love with you! You told me he was talking about marriage and buying you your dream house!"

"I know. But Fritzi . . . well, she's my first love."

Argh! I would want to grab these women by the shoulders, shake them like a rag doll, and scream some sense into them. *He's a MAN! He loves you! I wish I HAD A MAN LIKE THAT!* But I could only bite my tongue, force a smile, and walk away.

Fears

I know what was controlling Audrey: fear. After divorce we remember the devastation of being abandoned. We never forget the losses we had to work hard to recover from. We are consumed by a lack of faith and trust and allowing our fears to control us. Fears grow and multiply in the dark like mushrooms.

After divorce we can manage to rebuild a safe, quiet life. We've found we can be somewhat comfortable with the less we have now than we did before. Sure, we say we long for love and romance and possibly a new marriage—and in some sense we really do—but we don't yet have what it takes to go there. We also remember how much work a relationship takes! It just might be too difficult, too risky, and too painful. So we try to find a way to casually date or have sex or romance without the commitment that authentic love demands.

Read Kelly's story

After my divorce I dated Bill and we fell in love—or so I thought. He'd been divorced too, and his ex-wife had hired the toughest attorney in town. They wiped him out financially, and it took him ten years to rebuild a small but profitable one-man business. Eventually he bought a small house and had his two boys on weekends and Wednesdays. Bill liked routine and order, and he kept his house neat and clean. We went out every Friday night for pizza and watched TV on Sundays after church. He had a big dog, Annie, who curled up at the foot of his easy chair every night. Bill was loving to his boys and so sweet with that dog. That showed me his nurturing side.

But after a while, when I wanted to know where the relationship was going, he got nervous. We had plenty of chemistry, and I hoped we could make a go of it. After a few arguments, he finally came clean with me and said, "I'm sorry, but I have no plans for getting married, ever. I'll never let a woman and her attorney wipe me out like that again." I protested and asked, "But don't you miss love, romance, and intimacy?" His answer shocked me, but it made perfect sense. "I do miss it, but the price is too high. Besides, I have a nice home, a good business, my boys to keep me company, my dog to love me, and when I need sex, I have the Internet."

Poor Kelly . . . and poor Bill!

The story is crass, but it needs to be told. It is more common among the divorced than many realize. Fears of losing money, comfort, control, and freedom can keep us self-centered and unable to love.

On the other side the spectrum is fear of being alone and thus becoming too needy and clingy:

> Initially, my biggest fears were just getting through the divorce. Now, it's probably being old and being alone.
>
> —*Tricia*

What fears do you have? Maybe you could make a time one evening and start a list of fears you have in every area of your life. Add to it throughout the week as more come to mind. Examine which ones may be *real* versus *irrational*. Then take them to God in prayer and ask that He help you replace your fear with faith.

Your laundry list

Now that you have opened up your closet and the cellar doors, it's time to get rid of the mess that was hiding in there. Just as Bob took his mushroom-infested clothes to the laundry, we all need to take our sinful stuff to the cleaners. For Catholics, that would be the Sacrament of Reconciliation, or what we commonly call confession. Does that scare you?

If you're like many divorced people, you haven't been to confession in perhaps decades. You're not alone. In the next chapter I'll help you understand the beauty and power and freedom of the Sacrament, but first, your laundry list.

Those in the twelve-step programs call this a "searching and fearless moral inventory," and they are right: it requires digging all the way to the back of the closet and down into the cellar with the courage to face the fungi. Catholics call it an examination of conscience.

I usually write my sins down on a piece of paper and take it with me to confession. Some will tell you not to do that in case someone finds your list. But sometimes I have so many sins, little imperfections, and character defects that I *have* to bring that list. Just don't write your name and room number at the top like Sister Immaculata taught you and you'll be fine!

There are many ways to make a good and honest examination of conscience, and you can find them easily on the Internet. Some sins are more serious than others, but even the little ones can add up and become ingrained habits of selfishness. Our Catholic sacramental life affords us this regular "spring cleaning" not only to keep us smelling fresh and sweet but to free us to love God and others much more deeply.

If you haven't been to confession for a while, you may want to start by talking to your pastor or another wise and holy priest first. I like to start by reviewing where I have failed the Ten Commandments, which, yes, I memorized in third grade and still remember to this day. Do you?

Chapter 19

Learn to Love Your Laundry Room

IN your new life, your laundry room is the Catholic confessional, which used to be, and in some places still is, a small closet where you don't see the priest—and he doesn't see you.

In the last few decades, however, the Church has encouraged Her children to meet openly with the priest, face-to-face. Where you go to confession is your choice, but don't think one is better than the other. They both have benefits.

Going inside the closet

It's ironic that in the Sacrament of Reconciliation (confession), you go into the dark closets of your life to pull out the hidden mess and then go back into a "closet" to get rid of it. There's a good reason for that. When one is honest about their failings, a healthy shame follows. Shame is a sense that someone can now look upon our

sins and judge us, no longer seeing our inherent goodness and dignity. Sometimes we want to escape that
judicious gaze and hide to protect the gift of who we
are. Healthy shame is also an honest response that real-
izes and accepts our limitations. Going to confession in
the dark—behind a curtain—is a practice that has been
developed primarily to protect anonymity. Confessing
behind a curtain can help us feel less exposed, and the
anonymity can help us open up and confess freely and
fully.

But, for some, being in the dark can also feel oppres-
sive and trigger a fear of not being seen or valued. In
response to those who are unloving or condemning,
the culture has told us to get rid of all shame—healthy
or otherwise—promoting shamelessness instead. This
attitude rejects any notion of personal sin. Sounds good,
right? We can quickly buy into that lie because we hate
feeling guilty. However, instead of denying the guilt
and shame of sin—which leads to spiritual death—the
Church says, "Bring your dirty laundry here. Free wash
and dry, plus fluff and fold!"

Coming out into the open

Where going into the confessional can remind us of
the shame of sin, meeting the priest face-to-face helps
some realize that confession really is about bringing it
all out into the open. This reminds us that our sin, like

mushrooms, is killed in the blazing light of God's love and mercy.

Another benefit of the face-to-face posture is that some people may experience Jesus more fully with more of their senses. Jesus Christ is incarnate, meaning in the literal sense that He has a body like us, with real flesh-and-blood meat on His bones. The pure Spirit of God came to the world in Jesus, who is an embodied person—fully God and fully human. In confession, the priest is not operating in his own power, but in the person of Jesus. In a certain sense, the priest says to Christ the words we hear Christ say to us, "This is my body, given for you," so that now Jesus might have eyes to look into ours, lips to speak words of forgiveness and love, and hands to lay gently on us. In both face-to-face and anonymous confession, we are fully encountering Jesus through the priest, and the effects of the Sacrament are the same regardless of the approach. And both styles can produce deep emotional benefits. But many who have had the priest lay his hands gently on their head as they are absolved, or who have had the priest smile kindly at them, report a relief and release they didn't experience behind the curtain.

The potential drawback of this form of the Sacrament is to approach it in an overly casual and friendly manner, forgetting the serious nature of sin. You shake hands, sit down, and grin. "Hey, Father. How ya doin'? Nice shot on the golf course last week!" Even if you start with casual friendliness, hopefully the priest will gently bring you to a place of quiet reflection and respect for the Sacrament—a true encounter with the living God.

I love seeing the priest look me in the eyes with compassion and understanding. I love hearing him say, "I absolve you of your sins" as He speaks on behalf of Jesus Himself. Some priests will lay their hands on your head, and the physical touch that comes with the words of absolution can give you shivers of joy and bring tears of relief. Sometimes when I go to confession I go into the room with a heavy heart, but I leave crying with relief and laughing for joy at the same time.

—Margaret

I like the dark confessional. It's quiet and peaceful, and I am not distracted by any visual stimulation. I can close my eyes or simply peer dimly through the little screen and see the barest outline of Father. It reminds me that Jesus truly is as close to me as the priest is—I can hear him breathing—but the veil of this life still keeps us from the full, face-to-face glory we will have when we come home to heaven.

—Nate

Why we need the Sacrament

What we used to call the Sacrament of Penance is now called the Sacrament of Reconciliation, which better describes the healing encounter we have with Christ. When we sin, we lose God's grace and become weaker in our attempts to love Him and others. We'd sink to our death in our own sins if we could not admit we're drowning, reach out in repentance, and ask for God's forgiveness. When we do that, He is able to throw us a lifeline and restore grace to our souls. Grace helps us resist future sin and love God and others more.

God also promises to wipe away our sin forever—if we are truly sorry, confess as fully and honestly as we can, and are willing to make amends and try our best not to sin again. Scripture tells us He even forgets it and never holds it against us! Of course, we still may have to suffer some natural consequences for sin, as well as purification, but after Reconciliation, nothing keeps us from His love and life in our hearts.

Mortal and venial sins

Some modern "theologians" or others may tell you there is no such thing as sin. Please! Anyone who has been through a divorce knows that, yes, there certainly is hardness in the heart of mankind that kills the life of God's in the soul. Scripture tells us that some sins are more serious than others,[1] and common sense tells us that as well. The following is a helpful excerpt from Father Colin P. Donovan, expert on the Eternal Word Television Network (EWTN) website's Answers section.

A serious, grave or mortal sin is the knowing and willful violation of God's law in a serious matter, for example, idolatry, adultery, murder, slander. . . . Mortal sin is called mortal because it is the "spiritual" death of the soul (separation from God). If we are in the state of grace it loses this supernatural life for us. If we die without repenting we will lose Him for eternity. However, by turning our hearts back to Him and receiving the Sacrament of [Reconciliation] we are restored to His friendship. Catholics are not allowed to receive Communion if they have unconfessed mortal sins.

Venial sins are slight sins. They do not break our friendship with God, although they injure it. . . . It is always good to remember, especially those who are trying to be faithful but sometimes fall, that for mortal sin it must not only be 1) serious matter, but 2) the person must know it is serious and then 3) freely commit it. These two categories of sin are explicitly to be found in Sacred Scripture.[2]

I encourage you to learn more by visiting the EWTN website (www.ewtn.com) or *Catholic Answers* website (www.Catholic.com). Between these two faithful sites, there probably isn't a question about our faith you won't find answered in a way that's easy to understand—and in complete agreement with the *Catechism of the Catholic Church*.

How often should you go to confession?

The Church—our Mother—reminds us that if we have mortal sin, we must get to confession immediately. She loves us and doesn't want us to lose God's life in our souls! Otherwise, She recommends confession at least once a year, like spring cleaning. But I ask you this: if you deeply offended the one you dearly love, when and how often would you seek forgiveness and reconciliation? Right away and always, right? Don't wait a year.

Can't you just go directly to God instead of the priest?

Of course you can go directly to God and confess, and you should. That's what we do at the beginning of each Mass to make ourselves as sweet-smelling as possible when we intimately encounter our Lord in the Eucharist. In fact, the closer to God you get and the more aware of how often you fail to love Him more fully, the more you may be saying "I'm so sorry!" on a daily basis. These little acts of contrition are a good habit. But the Sacraments give us powerful graces we don't get otherwise. Jesus wants to give us those sanc-

> Jesus wants to give us those sanctifying graces to strengthen our minds and hearts and keep His divine life in us alive.

tifying graces to strengthen our minds and hearts and keep His divine life in us alive. He specifically established the Sacraments as the way to obtain those blessings. Thank God we have them!

Crucifying sin

Each one of the seven Sacraments, in some sense, is our participation with Jesus in His crucifixion and resurrection—where sin itself is crucified and dies and we rise with Christ to new life. This isn't just Church speak or theological babble—it is real. It works.

Bob hadn't been to confession for forty-five years.

I didn't really think I needed church; I had my own relationship with God and would often enjoy vigorous bike rides or hikes into the hills to commune with Him. It was genuine but, at the same time, a lazy faith where I connected with God when and how it suited me—or when I needed His help.

For decades I made myself master of my world. I was too smart for religion, and the ever-growing culture of narcissism backed me up. I bought into all the lies: religion was a crutch for the weak and the reason for atrocious wars. The Church was filled with disgusting hypocrites. The pope and all the clergy were pointy-hat misfits who couldn't hold a real job or know how to make love to a woman. Jesus and Buddha were pretty much the same, although I preferred the peacefulness that seemed to come from Buddhism over the Christian fanatics. I was sincere in my beliefs but grossly uninformed and arrogant as all hell. I prided myself on being a loner, outside tradition, and being way too cool for the masses. I realized later it was all part of a false-self I'd developed to survive the confusion and pain of a world—and a God I did not understand, didn't trust, and to whom I refused to submit.

I didn't even really think I sinned. I was simply a good person. No rape, murder, or grand-theft auto. But I had no idea how selfish I was and how I used other people on a daily basis in lots of little ways. But when I returned to Church I began to open up to God and had some profoundly mystical encounters with Christ in the Blessed Sacrament. My faith became real again. I started to understand that the wisdom and holiness of the men and women in the Church for the last two thousand years far surpassed the hypocrisy and wars that I had always been so quick to point out. God revealed to me quite clearly that I had been filled with pride and arrogance since my high-school years, and, yes, I had many sins. It blew me away. The scales started falling from my eyes and changes were happening almost daily.

I was coming home. But there was just one more thing—confession. Gulp!

Wash day!

When I first showed up back at the local parish for morning Mass, I thought the old priest would have a heart attack. Father hadn't seen me set foot in the church in a long time. His eyebrows raised to the ceiling, and in his Irish brogue he exclaimed, "Bob! Good Lord! The next thin' ya know, the roof'll be fallin' in on us all!" We laughed.

Soon after that I finally had the courage to

tell him I needed to go to confession—and that it had been forty-five years. He didn't blink an eye. I asked if I would be using the dark, secret confessional, and he quickly replied, "Oh no, Bob. Make an appointment and we'll sit down tagather and have a good hahrt-to-hahrt. Now go home and make a good examination of conscience."

I did. In his office, with my soul bared and my heart open, I poured out the arrogance I'd had for decades. We sat talking together for a long time and Father lovingly received my innermost heart. I came home lighter, freer . . . and truly forgiven. I know it was Christ who was listening to me and loving me. I know it was Him who forgave me.

Bob's story reveals the power of an intimate encounter with Christ through the eyes, ears, and heart of a priest. Mountaintop moments with God are good, but Sacraments are better.

Are you ready to clean up?

In case you haven't been to the Sacrament of Reconciliation for a while, here's an examination of conscience you can take with you to the confessional.

The Ten Commandments

First Commandment: *I am the LORD your God. You shall have no other gods before me.*

Have I . . .

◇ Knowingly disobeyed the commandments of God or the Church?

◇ Missed Mass intentionally on Sundays and Holy Days of obligation and rationalized it wasn't wrong?

◇ Failed to observe the prescribed days of fast and abstinence?

◇ Habitually came late to Mass or left early?

◇ Refused to accept Church teachings?

◇ Failed to go to confession once a year (for serious sin) or receive the Eucharist at Easter time?

◇ Been lazy about teaching my children to attend Mass and obey God?

◇ Ignored God or only kept Him on the back burner for emergencies?

◇ Failed to make my faith a top priority in my life?

◇ Been lazy about prayer or learning more about God and the Faith?

◇ Shopped around for a non-Catholic church because I felt I wasn't being "fed?"
◇ Joined or dabbled in another religion?
◇ Bargained or demanded things from God?
◇ Made other things (money, sex, people, etc.) a priority in my time, energy, and focus?
◇ Engaged in superstitious practices (daily horoscopes, tarot cards, etc.)?
◇ Been involved in the occult (séances, Ouija boards, etc.)?
◇ Hidden a serious sin?

Second Commandment: *You shall not take the name of the LORD your God in vain.*

Have I . . .

◇ Carelessly used the name of Jesus?
◇ Used the name of God in cursing or blasphemy?
◇ Failed to keep vows or promises that I have made to God?
◇ Spoken about God or the Church with arrogance or defiance?
◇ Committed perjury (breaking an oath or lying under oath)?

Third Commandment: *Remember the Sabbath day, to keep holy.*

Have I . . .

◇ Worked or done business unnecessarily on Sunday?

◇ Failed to make Sunday a day of true rest and spiritual recharging?

◇ Failed to observe the Communion fast (not eating or drinking within one hour of receiving Communion—other than for medical need)?

Fourth Commandment: *Honor your father and your mother.*

Have I . . .

◇ Disrespected or disparaged my parents in any way?

◇ Born resentment, unforgiveness, or hatred toward my parents—dead or alive?

◇ Failed to pray for my parents?

◇ Neglected the needs of my parents in their old age or in their time of need?

◇ Not lived in humble obedience to those who legitimately exercise authority over me?

Fifth Commandment: *You shall not kill.*

Have I . . .

◇ Unjustly and intentionally killed someone's spirit with my words or actions?

◇ Purposely provoked another by teasing or nagging?

◇ Verbally or emotionally abused another person?

◇ Deliberately wished or prayed that someone were dead?

◇ Indulged in serious anger or rage?

◇ Hated another person or wished him evil?

◇ Been mean to, quarreled with, or willfully hurt someone?

◇ Been unforgiving to others when mercy or pardon was requested?

◇ Sought revenge or hoped something bad would happen to someone?

◇ Delighted to see someone else suffer or get hurt?

◇ Been involved in an abortion, directly or indirectly (through advice, etc.)?

◇ Seriously considered or attempted suicide?

◇ Supported, promoted, or encouraged the practice of assisted suicide or mercy killing?

◇ Unjustly threatened or hurt someone physically?

◇ Been prejudiced or unjustly discriminated against others?

◇ Recklessly endangered my life or health, or that of another, by my actions?

◇ Driven recklessly or under the influence of alcohol or other drugs?

◇ Abused alcohol, food, or drugs?

◇ Sold or given drugs to others to use for non-therapeutic purposes?

◇ Helped another to commit a serious sin (through advice or encouragement)?

Sixth and Ninth Commandments: *You shall not commit adultery. You shall not covet your neighbor's wife.*

Have I . . .

◇ Been lazy about or failed to learn what the Church teaches about sexuality?

◇ Looked upon another, even a spouse, selfishly and as an object for my sexual pleasure?

◇ Rejected any Church teachings on matters of sexual morality?

◇ Withheld the gift of my fertility from my spouse by contraception?

◇ Refused to receive the gift of children from God without just and serious reasons?

◇ Used my or another's body outside the marital act (in vitro fertilization or artificial insemination) so I could get children?

◇ Sterilized myself for contraceptive purposes?

◇ Withheld myself sexually from a spouse out of anger, hurt, control, or revenge?

◇ Pushed myself sexually on my spouse, or another, without loving concern?

◇ Deliberately caused male climax outside of normal sexual intercourse?

◇ Purchased, viewed, or made use of pornography—even soft core?

◇ Failed to choose appropriate movies and television programs?

◇ Listened to music or jokes that are harmful to purity?

◇ Had sex outside marriage?

◇ Trained myself in selfish sexual behavior by masturbating?

◇ Engaged in sexual foreplay reserved for marriage?

◇ Engaged in unnatural sexual activities?

◇ Engaged in prostitution or paid for the services of a prostitute?

◇ Seduced someone or allowed myself to be seduced?

◇ Made uninvited and unwelcome sexual advances toward another?

◇ Purposely dressed immodestly?

Seventh and Tenth Commandments: *You shall not steal. You shall not covet your neighbor's house.*

Have I . . .

◇ Been seriously jealous of another for any reason?

◇ Stolen someone's possessions, money, or time?

◇ Cheated a teacher, an employer, the government, or anyone else?

◇ Failed to pay my employees fairly and generously?

◇ Failed to honor a business contract?

◇ Failed to pay a debt?

◇ Been too attached to possessions?

◇ Refused to be generous with others?

◇ Not handled my money wisely?

◇ Deliberately defaced or destroyed another's property?

◇ Made a false claim to an insurance company?

◇ Overcharged someone, especially to take advantage of another's hardship or ignorance?

Eighth Commandment: *You shall not bear false witness against your neighbor.*

Have I . . .

◇ Lied in any way?
◇ Gossiped?
◇ Willfully deceived others or withheld information they needed?
◇ Told lies about another person in order to destroy his or her reputation?
◇ Failed to make reparation for a lie I told or for harm done to a person's reputation?
◇ Failed to speak out in defense of the Catholic Faith, the Church, or another person?
◇ Betrayed another's confidence?

Just for the divorced:

Have I . . .

◇ Left a valid marriage without just cause (grave abuse or danger)?
◇ Caused undue hardship, stress, or abuse on a spouse to cause them to leave?
◇ Failed within the marriage to get counseling or take other action that may have helped?
◇ Remarried outside the Church?
◇ Continued to receive the Sacraments of Reconciliation or Holy Communion after

remarrying outside the Church?

◇ Sought a priest who would overlook Church teachings to accommodate me?

◇ Followed advice of a lay person or clergy that I knew was against Church teaching?

◇ Lied or caused others to lie in my annulment petition?

◇ Lied or deliberately misled others in the divorce proceedings to gain greater property, possessions, or even time with the children?

◇ Bad-mouthed my former spouse to my children or others?

◇ Tried to alienate my children's affection from their other parent?

◇ Failed to pay court-ordered or just child or spousal support?

◇ Failed to honor the court settlement agreement?

◇ Failed to honor the visitation agreement?

◇ Refused to be generous in the children's visitation with their other parent?

◇ Refused to be open, honest, and communicative with my former spouse in post-divorce dealings?

◇ Withheld forgiveness from or harbored bitterness toward my ex-spouse?

◇ Deliberately tried to sabotage his or her new relationships?
◇ Harbored bitterness or resentment toward someone at church who rejected or hurt me because of my divorce?

Chapter 20

Make the Kids' Room Safe

ARE you a better parent now after the divorce? Divorce has a way of shaking people up in all areas, including parenting. It's so easy while we're married to get caught up in daily details and regular routines as the kids just keep growing taller and getting older. Before you know it they are asking you to take them down to the DMV to get their driver's licenses! No one should have to go through divorce to improve on parenting skills, but divorce can make us look long and hard at the most important areas of life—our children, for one—and spur us to make much-needed changes.

Let's see what some divorced parents had to say about parenting before and after a divorce:

> I think I was always a great dad to my two kids. But I think the divorce made me an even better dad because it made me realize how precious my time is with my kids and that I should

make the best of every single moment I have with them.

—Jeff

Other than what you see growing up, no one really teaches you how to be a parent. In high school they make you take driver's ed. but not parenting ed. I'd been a bit lax on educating myself about my own children and how to raise them. Immediately after the divorce, I read several books on parenting. I also joined a couple of Internet groups that give parenting advice.

—Marissa

I was always busy on weekends working with the yard, working in the garage, and watching sports on television. Not that I intentionally ignored my kids, but it was easier to stay busy with other things since their mother was in the house to keep an eye on them. I don't do all that anymore. On the weekends I have my children I spend much more one-on-one time with them. I hate to admit it, but that came as a result of the divorce!

—Brett

I didn't move. My ex moved. She moved into a condo in another city. We were in the midst of construction—adding two bedrooms and a bathroom to a 1920s-era Spanish revival home. . . . My wife left me holding all the bags, financial and otherwise, including finishing the room additions on our house. I didn't want to move because I wanted to keep our kids in their same bedrooms and maintain some level of continuity in their lives. On the other hand, I couldn't move if I wanted to. I couldn't sell the house until the room additions were completed and the city signed off on the inspections. I initially fumed about it as I spent countless hours painting and making other repairs on my own. But in time I realized all this was a blessing. Having all that work to do distracted me from too much focus on the incredible pain I was feeling. I also felt good about my accomplishments in home improvement and the fact that I was able to do so many things on my own. I also felt good about keeping my kids' home intact. I even built them a tree house in the backyard. Sometimes for fun we would have dinner in that tree house.

—Jeff

Once you've lost a spouse or a house, the fear of losing the kids can come next. It can motivate you to do whatever you have not been doing before to be a better parent. Maybe you need to start with praying a little bit more. My sister Barb told me:

The kids are great—because their God was/
is always at their side. I did a lot of things [to be
a good parent], but I think the most important
was that I used to tell my guardian angel to be
sure the kids' guardian angels did a good job!

Diane wrote me a painful email about praying after
a divorce:

I was so teary-eyed yesterday! With the
holidays approaching and funds so low, I hate
being divorced! My daughter (who is nine) is
a new altar server at church. And her dad and
his sister came to see her at Mass. . . . As we
pulled out of the church parking lot, my daughter and I were talking about our prayers. And
she said, "Mommy, I prayed again that Daddy
would come home to you, me, and Paige." Oh,
it kills me.

What do you say to that? If you're grounded in what
I call the big-picture truths, you can respond well to the
kids' questions or comments. Here are some basic big-
picture teachings that are paraphrased from the teachings in the *Catechism of the Catholic Church*. You can post
them on the fridge and use them for family discussion,
asking the children to share some times they have seen
these principles at work:

◇ Life is really fun and wonderful—and really
   hard and sad at the same time.

◇ God has the best home for us in Heaven—with Him—and that's the one we need to keep our eye on.

◇ God lets people make free choices, and that means bad or unfair things might happen to good people—like us!

◇ God loves us more than anything and promises to be with us during those hard, unfair, and painful times.

◇ God promises He will bring some surprisingly good things out of bad things if we love Him and are patient.

◇ When you love someone, you will bear suffering as Jesus did for us. Good things can come from that even though we can't see it right now.

If you're a single parent

While it may feel like you're rearing your children all alone, no one is really a single parent—every child has a mother and a father, even if one is absent or deceased. After divorce, mothers and fathers must remember that their children do have another parent, as imperfect as he or she is and as infrequent as that parent may appear in the kids' lives. It's just that some parents after divorce have the majority or entire burden of the day-to-day raising of the children—or feel like they do.

On his radio broadcast, Dr. James Dobson of *Focus on the Family* often said, "Single-parenting is the toughest job in the universe."

But that is not cause for self-pity or sustained anger. If you're rebuilding a life alone—that is, without another loving adult in the home to assist you—get some help. What if you and your kids had just been in a terrible car accident and were all lying in the street bleeding to death? Would you crawl around on the pavement holding one hand to your own bloodied wounds and tend to your children all by yourself as bystanders watched at a distance? No! You'd be hollering, "Help me, please! Help us!" And people—even total strangers—would sense your need and rush to help as best they could. After divorce, families carry internal emotional wounds. The average person in your family or community may not sense the needs you and your family have. Please get over any false sense of pride that may be keeping you isolated or alone as a parent. Call out—loudly if necessary—to family, friends, and neighbors. Ask your pastor if he can find you some help. Call up the ladies' guild at Church. Ask the men's group if they can help you fix the car. See if someone in the

> If you're rebuilding a life alone—that is, without another loving adult in the home to assist you—get some help.

youth group is a certified babysitter. Call for an "Amish" family-raising!

Some rebuilding tips

I assume that most of you reading this book have already stabilized things in some of the basic crisis areas, especially with your children. Praying for and spending more time with the children is good, but if you want to continue to help the kids after a divorce, consider some of these other practical rebuilding tips—suitable for both young kiddies and adult children!

Nail down your primary goal

Everyone wants their child to be healthy, happy, and successful. But your job as a parent is not to help get the kids to Harvard; it's to help get them to Heaven. Period. If you can remember this one goal, it will help you focus on what is really important and set aside what is not.

Pick a patron saint

Remind the kids that saints are real and that they are more alive now than they ever were. They love to ask favors from God for those who call on them in prayer. Get a book of saints and tell your children to spend a week going through it and picking their own personal patron saint. You pick one too. One night at dinner you can all share who you picked and why. On birthdays, Christmas, and other occasions, buy simple statues, plaques, or medals of their saint so they can start a collection.

Keep working on your own flaws first

You know the standard warning given while travelling in an airplane with your children; in case of emergency, you MUST put on your own oxygen mask first or you'll be no help to the kids. If you are still hobbling around in anger, depression, misery, or confusion after your divorce, you can actually delay everyone's healing or even make it worse. Get a therapist, a spiritual director, or even a medical doctor if necessary. Ask God to show you what needs to be done.

Teach them what you learn

You are your child's primary teacher, and you know better than anyone how to speak their language. Unless your child needs special or unusual treatment that only a doctor or a psychologist can provide, *you* can help them heal. Share with them every valuable principle you learn in therapy, read in a book, or hear in a sermon. You don't have to be a natural teacher. Just make some quiet time at dinner or in the car on a road trip and talk together. Talk some more. Talk again later. Ask questions and share stories. They need to hear you. They need to know you.

Acknowledge their pain

We're all guilty at one time or another of rushing in when someone cries or gets angry and telling them, "Stop," "It will be okay," "Don't feel that way," or "You'll be fine—just give it time." Don't do that anymore. Learn instead to really *listen* and then say things like:

"Wow, honey, I didn't know you were so sad. Do you need a hug?"

"I totally understand your anger! I'd be upset, too. Can I help you in any way?"

"I hate being depressed too. Is there something I can do to make it better?"

"I get lonely too. Let's watch a movie, take a walk, or play a game."

Humor helps in healing hurts, but you have to be careful that it doesn't come across as glib or that you are discounting their feelings. Get to know your child's temperament, and you'll know if they need cheering up or if they just need you to sit with them in their misery for a while.

Answer their questions

No question should be off limits. Parents need to be the place where kids can safely come and get the hard questions answered. But that doesn't mean your eight-year-old gets the whole low-down on the dirty details of the finances or the affair that broke up your family. It may be tempting to bad-mouth your ex-spouse or someone else, especially in a mixed message sent to them in "saintly" terms. Don't do that.

The words the kids hear you say: "Daddy is a good man and we love him, but he listened to Satan and now our family is all broken. We must pray for him to be good again. Dear Jesus, bless Daddy."

The message they might really hear you say: "Your father is a very bad man who has done a very bad thing. He is filled with the devil. Something is really wrong with him, and he ruined our lives. Thank God we're not like that! Let's ask God to make Daddy good like us."

This thinly veiled arrogance makes your children afraid and unsettled and may cause them to harbor anger or bitterness toward their own father. Go higher. Ask God for the grace to forgive, have peace, and teach your children only love, forgiveness, and trust in Him. Keep working at it.

What you should say: "I'm not sure of all the reasons Daddy isn't here now, and I'm working with God to figure it all out. This is a tough time, isn't it? But don't worry. Whatever happens, we both love you. When you pray tonight, will you ask God to help Daddy and me be good and do the right thing? God will always take care of *all* of us. Always. Let's thank Him right now!"

Balance their schedule

The old saying "Idle hands are the devil's workshop" means hanging around with nothing useful to do will tempt some to sinful activity. But our culture is on the other end of the spectrum, going insane with busyness and hyperactivity. Activity distracts us so we don't have to stop and experience the sometimes painful reality of life. Limit your kids to one sport or activity per season, and maybe *none* for a few months. Turn off the TV and the computer and encourage the kids to read a good book. Ignore their complaints.

Don't become their best buddy

Friendship is a dimension of any loving relationship, but your kids *have* friends. They don't need you to be their best buddy. Instead they need an adult parent to teach, guide, and push them to "go higher" in life, even if it temporarily makes them angry or disappointed in you. When there is a big, empty emotional hole in a parent's heart and the parent thinks he or she needs the child's love to fill that hole, it sets mom or dad up to fall into this trap of loving a child in an overly-attached way that is very close to using them. Love people and use things, not the other way around.

Reclaim your authority

God gave you a share in His authority to get your kids—His kids, really—to Heaven. Too many parents abdicate this gift from God after a divorce because they think the kids need a rest from anything too difficult, like obedience! Just say no. Your kids need that guidance from you. If you can't say no, ask God to show you why you fear the loss of their approval and affection for you. Maybe you have the mistaken belief that a good parent makes kids happy. The truth is that a good parent helps kids be holy.

Monitor their friendships

When children are young, you must take a firm stance and insist they stop seeing certain playmates who are not good friends. As they get older, however, you'll want to help them take inventory, assess friendships, and make that decision for themselves. Don't be afraid to start—and even continue—a discussion by saying something like, "Honey, I know you like Gina, but I'm not sure she's the best friend for you right now because _____. This divorce taught me that we all need to take a good look at what we have brought into our lives and make sure it pleases God. That way we build our home on the rock that the Bible tells us about. Let's talk about how we can rebuild together. What do you think?" In the end, using your own good judgment, you may still need to halt the relationship. Tell them the stories in this book, like the one about Hugo having to come clean out the rats. Their life is like a house too. They'll understand.

Don't make them a surrogate spouse

Sometimes parents overstep natural boundaries and make their children an emotional surrogate spouse.

We're aghast at the very thought of unnatural sexual relations, but sometimes a deeply emotional relationship with a child can be as damaging in a different way. It's tempting to fill the empty spot your spouse left with a child who is dear to your heart. You've seen them—fathers who are too close to their daughters, mothers to their sons. They sit and talk for hours about subjects that are too adult for the child. They may go everywhere together. The parent cries on the child's shoulder, and the child comforts him or her. I'm not talking about normal and healthy isolated times of comfort and companionship. If you think you may have leaned a bit too much on a child after your divorce, ask God for the insight and grace to bring balance to the situation.

Be generous with visitation time

Unless their other parent is a true danger to them, be generous with visitation time, even when it is not spelled out in the agreement. My father always told us, "The best thing a father can do for his children is to love their mother." The same is true after a divorce. You don't have to trust or feel affection for the other parent to be generous. And a new saying for our divorced culture might be, "The best thing a father or mother can do for the children is let them love the other parent."

Help them dream dreams and set goals

It's never too early to teach your kids how to dream and set goals for themselves. It's a confidence booster and a building (or rebuilding) tool they'll need to take with them into adulthood. Maybe your children are adults but they never learned this; you might still be a good influence by asking the questions, "What are your dreams?" "Do you have a plan how to get there?" and "How can I help you make a plan?" A simple start is asking your children what they would like to have. When they say "a Porsche," just laugh! Don't do it for them, but help them to pick something realistic, research the best price, make a list of chores they could do to earn money, and make a budget. They will not forget this if you follow through with them.

Make them do hard things

Many marriages fail because people just don't want to work hard at anything anymore. No one wants to suffer, so we self-medicate or run instead. This attitude starts in childhood when a kid whines and mommy or daddy rushes in to fix it, clean it, or buy it. In our culture there is a phenomenon of extended adolescence—emotionally we're all stuck in a self-centered teenage mode even though we advance in age into our twenties, thirties, forties, and beyond. Parents who don't lovingly but firmly push their kids into adulthood are turning out future weak and selfish spouses who fear the hard work and commitment required of marriage.

Where are you still doing the work your children could be doing? Did you know you may be depriving them of the "muscles" needed for maturity? Quit waking them up in the morning; buy an alarm clock and show them how to use it. Let them be late and walk to school and home again. They can make their own breakfast and pack a lunch. Make them finish the chore even when it takes a long time or gets difficult. Fire the gardener and put the kids to work. Even youngsters should be picking up clothes and belongings, putting them away, making beds, doing or helping with laundry, and turning off the TV when you tell them to. You are training them to be responsible and self-giving husbands or wives someday soon, and their future spouse will thank you!

> Parents who don't lovingly but firmly push their kids into adulthood are turning out future weak and selfish spouses who fear the hard work and commitment required of marriage.

Teach them the Faith

What do you want most for your children? Many divorced parents tell me they just want their children to be happy (again). But we must lift our eyes higher and remember this life is not our true home. The culture is already trying to seduce your children into thinking that being happy here and now is the most important thing. More than anything, don't you really want your child in Heaven for all eternity? Then don't just drop them off at the church for class; parents, not the CCD instructors, are children's primary teachers of the Faith. Kids need to both learn the facts of the Faith and see you loving and living it. So love it, live it, and pass it on.

Work yourself out of a job

I once heard it said that your job as a parent is to work yourself out of job. That means that as they get older, they should need less protection and more preparation. By the time they are seventeen or eighteen, the age they can go off to war, you should have your hands completely off those training wheels in nearly every area. Your children should be ready to stand on their own two feet and go out into the world—not marry the first person who comes along so they can have a bigger apartment, more disposable income, and someone to take care of them. That's a recipe for divorce.

Help them learn to fly

In several places in Scripture, God uses the image of a soaring eagle to teach the spiritual truth of how He keeps us safe and wants to show us how to "fly." Since parents share in the Fatherhood of God, there is parenting wisdom for us in this verse:

> Like an eagle that stirs up its nest, that flutters over its young, spreading out its wings, catching them, bearing them on its pinions.
> —Deuteronomy 32:11

Eagles make their nests in the high places, in the secure cleft of the rock. The rock points parents to the solid foundation on which we must build, or in this case rebuild, our lives and homes: Christ.

The eagle builds the nest with sticks and stones for shape and form but lines it with downy feathers for the baby eaglets' comfort. That's what we do in making our home warm and comfy for our kids.

Now what baby would ever want to leave the nest and learn to fly with such soft, comfortable surroundings? So every day the parent eagle stirs up the nest just a bit each day to slowly remove the "warm fuzzies" and introduce the reality of sharp sticks and stones. As the nest becomes less comfortable, the chicks are motivated to leave and try their wings. But we get it wrong when we do too much and give too much to our children, refusing to let them suffer or preparing them to "fly" into the world.

The parent eagle flies closely around the nest, showing the eaglets how to fly. Our children can never rebuild after divorce until we first begin to rebuild. They won't know how to fly in life unless we are first flying strong and true. We need to be able to say, "Watch me!"

The eagle hovers closely, ready to catch the baby should it fall on its first attempts. Just as our loving Father God is there to catch us but always calling us to go higher, parents too should *protect* but *push* at the same time.

As soon as one of the baby eagles catches the wind and begins to soar on its own, the others watch from the nest and are motivated and assured that they too can fly. Out they jump, one by one. You and I can get our motivation from others who have done it right. Our children will be motivated by watching us and others too. That's why we need to fill our homes with good friends and family who have made their nest in the cleft of a solid Rock and are flying high.

Let Him be the wind beneath your wings

I know parenting can be exhausting, even in a good marriage. After divorce, one hardly has the energy left to do anything, much less take care of all the things we should be doing for our kids. Our broken homes are a lot like those stirred-up nests: divorce blew away the downy feathers and the rocks and sticks began to poke us mercilessly, forcing us to jump.

But if you will rebuild your life in the cleft of the Rock of Ages, you will find shelter. He will show *you* (and you can show the kids) how to fly like you never have before, with the powerful wind of the Holy Spirit beneath your wings, lifting you up to new heights in God. That's His promise in Isaiah 40:28–31:

> Have you not known? Have you not heard? The LORD is the everlasting God, the Creator of the ends of the earth. He does not faint or grow weary, his understanding is unsearchable. He gives power to the faint, and to him who has no might he increases strength. Even youths shall faint and be weary, and young men shall fall exhausted; but they who wait for the LORD shall renew their strength, they shall mount up with wings like eagles, they shall run and not be weary, they shall walk and not faint.

Chapter 21

Enjoy Your Living Room

"COMPANY's coming! Can you please straighten up the living room?" Part of rebuilding will be inviting others into your life for intimate sharing, food, and fun. But what if you're too depressed, tired, or even afraid?

After divorce a certain period of isolation may be just what you need to lick your wounds and allow God to heal your broken heart. And even after you start to feel better, there may be times where you have to go back into isolation to recenter yourself. That's normal for any person. Remember how Jesus would sometimes leave everyone and go away by Himself? But ultimately you were made for relationships, and after divorce you must reassess and rebuild friendships.

Building right relationships

Relationships are where you are able to *give* of yourself, a necessity for true holiness and happiness.

Relationships are also where you can *receive* abundant blessings from God—through the eyes, ears, arms, and lips of others. Here are some tips for relationship building:

Clear your calendar for your friends

Some people find a temporary sense of security, comfort, and distraction from pain in work and excess activity. That doesn't leave time for cultivating healthy friendships. Turn off the TV or computer and call a friend. Make time for cards, coffee, a walk, whatever.

Get on Facebook, but get off Facebook

Social media is a great way to stay in touch, but it cannot substitute for the in-person time that we all need. How many hours a day are you on the computer? It may be way too much.

Be discriminating

People *can* have too many friends. In our culture there is barely enough time for work, sleep, prayer, dinner, and doing the laundry, much less the time required to nurture relationships. When my dad was in his nineties, he told me, "Rosie, looking back I can say that I could count my truest friends on one hand. No one needs more than that. No one has time for more than that! This life is over in a flash."

Learn to say no to the invitations that pull you in too many directions and especially to the friendships that are not good for you. Just as you jettison junk after a divorce, God may be asking you to jettison companionship that does not build you up and encourage holiness. It is not unkind, mean, or unchristian to learn to say goodbye.

—◇—

People *can* have too many friends. In our culture there is barely enough time for work, sleep, prayer, dinner, and doing the laundry, much less the time required to nurture relationships.

—◇—

After divorce I lost a lot of friends. It made me re-evaluate what true friendship was, and I realized I had a lot of acquaintances who were not good for me. We may have shared good things in common—like work, church, or hobbies—but some would bend the rules or even break the law. My long-time buddy was a great guy with a good heart but a big pot-smoker who often complained bitterly about the Church. I decided it was time to close the door on anything that would be a negative in my life. I told him I was trying to rebuild my life and, because of new things going on with me, would not have time to hang out anymore. I thanked him for being my friend all these years. I felt a little weird, but afterward I felt great. I knew I'd done the right thing.

—*Mark*

My girlfriend always disliked my husband and told me to leave him. She never advised me to get counseling or try to work it out. "Dump the guy" was her constant mantra. We'd been pals and bowling buddies for over fifteen years, so I hated ending the friendship. Turns out, he left me! But I knew it would not be good to harbor bitterness to him, and she only would have encouraged that in me. I stopped seeing her.

—*Chelsea*

Make your house a home

The way we set up our physical home can point to what's going on in our hearts. Is your house a chaotic mess, or is it warm and inviting? Do people love to come sit in your living room, or is it so perfect that the kids are not permitted on the sofa?

Growing up . . . I lived in a house where my brother and I were not allowed in the living room other than to clean it. If we were allowed to watch television, we had to lie on the adjacent dining room floor to watch.

—*Pat*

When I was a child, the living room was warm and a great place to read. I can remember cuddling up next to one of the radiators with a good book and being perfectly happy.

—*Judy*

Even if you have little to no energy after a divorce—or think that your physical environment is not important—stop to think about the last time you walked into church. It was probably decorated with special dishes, candlesticks, good smells, and flower arrangements. These things reinforce the holy and welcoming environment of a church.

Bring out the china, light the candles, play some music. Pick some flowers or greenery, put a colorful fabric on the table, or hang an interesting picture. These small steps can help make your physical environment feel safe and homey again.

Start new traditions

Thanksgiving, Christmas, and New Years are the time of year for warm welcomes, food, and fun. But divorce can shatter family traditions. You can start new ones, and I suggest you do.

I ended up at a Chinese restaurant on Christmas Eve with friends who had invited me to tag along. They had a tradition where they decided they'd worked hard all the week before Christmas and had already been to many parties and hosted several dinners. Since the next day they were starting over again with a big prime rib dinner for the family, they were ready to be waited on and eat something besides turkey, ham, and fruit cake. I hated being the fifth wheel, but the food was delicious and the restaurant was beautiful. I had a great time, and to this day I go out for Chinese dinner on Christmas Eve. I love it.

—*Maggie.*

One thing I had to do the first year was get new Christmas decorations. I couldn't bear to look at all the decorations my ex-wife and I had built up over the years because they brought back too many memories. It was all too much for me. So I asked my kids to go through the decorations and pick out the ones they wanted to take to their mom's house. Fortunately, they picked the ones that were the most emotion laden for me. So that worked out fine. My mom also brought us several boxes of her more recent decorations, which was great because they didn't conjure up any memories or emotions on my part. My kids and I have since developed a tradition of purchasing Christmas decoration souvenirs from the places we visit on our travels. I've taken them on several trips, so we now have a tree full of new memories—memories of great trips we've taken together since the divorce.

—Jeff

I remember shocking myself the first Christmas after [the] divorce. I always had the most gorgeous tree and mantle decorations. My ex left me in September, and I was still in shock and deep mourning when December hit. I did not get a tree for the first time in my life! Not one decoration. I went to Mass, thanked God for Baby Jesus, and came home and took a nap. It's okay not to do Christmas in the same way you always used to. As long as you remember the real reason for the season—Jesus. A few years later I started decorating again for the holidays, but I don't go over the top anymore.

—Elizabeth

Now during the holidays I simply celebrate with friends and enter more deeply into the spiritual side of it. I do not decorate my house in any way—very different from before. It's okay now.

—*P.R.*

Because Christmas was my ex's birthday, he got [the kids] on Christmas Day every year. We'd wake up, quickly do presents, and instead of being able to lounge around in our pajamas, eat Christmas cookies and candy, and play games, I'd have to pack them all up to send to his house. It was very emotionally difficult for me to have my kids' Christmas split here and there. So OUR favorite family holiday became Thanksgiving—and it has been ever since.

—*Theresa*

We have no problem with this. My ex-wife gets the kids Christmas Eve and has them Christmas morning. Then she brings them over to my mom's house around noon on Christmas Day, where we always celebrate Christmas. Then I have the kids for the rest of the day. I really like it like that.

—*Jeff*

The holidays, and our expectations of them, can be inordinate attachments. If you still have resentments, maybe even after decades, you probably need to reevaluate your priorities and get yourself to confession.

It was, and still is, after the divorce thirty years ago, a real struggle to get together at holiday time with my children. They have never completely accepted any residence I have lived in—always wishing for that Rockwell version of coming home to the house they were raised in for the holidays. Even though we are on good terms with my children, my [new] husband and I for the last few years have gone south for Christmas alone.

—Charlene

Go out by yourself

I'll never forget the first time I went to the movies alone after divorce. I felt awkward and embarrassed, but I forced myself to do it. I thought, *Just try it once, Rose, and if you hate it, you don't have to go again. At least you'll be able to say you did it!* I did not feel like going, but I moved with an act of the will to the local multiplex theater. I bought some buttered popcorn and a diet Coke (the dieter's oxymoron) and walked in to find a seat before the lights went down. I scanned the crowd and saw my associate pastor sitting all alone. *Wow! Father goes to the movies.* I never thought about that. He was a shy man, and I didn't really know him. But I thought *what-the-heck*. I moved to the seat next to him, sat down, and said "Hi Father! I'm Rose Sweet! Want some popcorn?" He smiled warmly, shook my hand, and politely shook his head no at my offer to share. We sat in silence for a few minutes, and then the movie started. On the way out he asked me how I enjoyed the movie, and then we each went home. Not much of a conversation, but every time I saw him after that at Mass, I'd make a point of saying "Hi, Father" and he'd smile and nod. He left a few years later, and I never saw him again. But I will never forget how relieved I felt at finding someone I knew that first time out on my own. Since then, I often go alone to the theater and love it.

Here's what other divorced men and women had to say about going out alone:

> About once a year I used to go to a local restaurant with a paperback book, order a before-dinner drink, an appetizer, full courses, dessert, and an after-dinner drink. It helped remind me of who I am.
>
> —*Barb*

> I never used to eat in restaurants by myself. But after the divorce, I started branching out and going to some of my favorite restaurants. Why not? I'd take a magazine or some of my

notes with me. I'm a writer, so I'm always writing outlines, organizing my thoughts, or reading. At first, it seemed odd. But after a while, I noticed that there were a lot of other single people doing it too. I also find that I like being surrounded by people and simply hearing the hustle and bustle of people talking.

—Jeff

I have never gone to the movies by myself and can't see myself doing that. That is a dating or family activity in my mind, and I can't see doing it alone!

—Sarah

It was Valentine's Day, and after a few years of being divorced, I was sick of being alone. I'd been telling divorced men and women in our recovery group they needed to venture out and try solo dining, but I had never done it myself. So I decided to go alone to an upscale seafood restaurant on the oceanfront and watch the sunset. I ordered a delicious steak dinner, a glass of expensive wine, and dessert. I toasted to God, thanking Him for the food, the sunset, and life in general—feeling content and happy. But then I looked around at all the romantic couples and realized I was the only single person there. My heart sunk, and I couldn't wait to get home. When I did, I burst into tears. I felt like Peter, who was walking on water when he had his eyes on God but sunk when he started looking around. That's a good lesson: keep your eyes on Him and you'll "walk on water." Look down, or around, and you could drown in sorrow and self-pity.

Chapter 22

Equip Your Garage

My dad had a tool shop on the side of the garage. Every weekend he'd be in there smoking his cigar and fixing something for Mom, and he'd suddenly stop and call me in.

"Rosie, go get your brothers and sisters." His voice was stern, and I knew what had happened—again.

In a few minutes all my siblings, plus a half dozen of our neighborhood playmates, would be lined up in a long row by height, our arms at our sides, staring obediently into Dad's face.

"I'm going to ask you kids each a question, and I want an honest answer. Okay?"

"Okay," we all replied in unison. He started with me, the oldest.

"Rosie, did you take my hammer?"

"Not me, Dad."

"Barbara, did you take my hammer?"

"Not me, Dad."

"Serena, did you . . ."

My father went down the long line, asking each child by name if he or she'd been the culprit. We all said, "Not me, Dad." When the last, Fred, who was still in diapers, would squeak out, "Nah me, Dada," my father's face would grow bright red with anger and you could see cigar smoke coming out of his ears!

"Then WHO TOOK MY HAMMER?"

Again a chorus of "Not me, not me, not me."

Finally Dad would surmise, "Well, I guess it just grew legs and WALKED OUT."

He'd calm down and turn back to his workbench, and we'd all quickly scurry away like cockroaches when the light goes on. Years later, when we were all adults, we told Dad it was always Charlie, the oldest boy, but my brother would have beaten us up if we ratted.

"That's what I figured." Dad told us, laughing at the memory.

You can't rebuild without tools

The garage of your life is where you keep your tools! No job is completed, or done properly, without the proper tools. Some people have no tools; others can't find them because there is just too much junk in there! Others are too afraid or overwhelmed to go digging in the giant mess.

My garage was ALWAYS super organized up until my home now. It's filled with real estate signs and just a lot of stuff. Stuff that I really should organize, donate, whatever. I just can't seem to get there for the first time in my life. Oh well! My priorities have certainly changed. After divorce, I find I am no longer Ms. Perfect.

—*P. R.*

The price paid for my current status is that any other tools bestowed upon me by our Creator have been lost inside the emotional and spiritual garage of my life, so unfamiliar and also unrecognizable that only a sense of fear accompanies any thought of trying to dust them off and use them now.

—*J. J.*

I want you to take a quick inventory of your home right now and make a mental list of all the tools you might have in your garage or other utility areas of the house:

◇ garden tools
◇ kitchen tools
◇ sewing tools
◇ household tools
◇ automotive tools
◇ craft tools

I bet you also have a library of reference manuals that show you how to operate or troubleshoot various appliances:

◇ cars
◇ computers
◇ televisions
◇ sewing machines
◇ stoves and ovens
◇ coffeemakers
◇ refrigerators
◇ smartphones
◇ bicycles
◇ toys

Okay. You've done well in making sure your physical life is adequately covered, but tell me, what tools and reference manuals do you have for your mental, emotional, and spiritual life? Why won't we spend the same time and money on tools to fix and build our interior life so that it is well-oiled and running smoothly?

Finding and fixing the fun in your life

After building a solid foundation in Christ and a life that is reasonably secured against the major aftershocks of divorce, you'll probably want to focus on these three major areas of rebuilding: your purpose, your personality, and your passion. You'll need some tools to help you get there. This book is one. After you read it, don't stick it in a box and store it in the garage. You'll never find it again to give to that divorced friend who may also need some rebuilding tools!

Your purpose

Discovering the purpose that drives your life has been the subject of many *New York Times* best-selling books and is a trend that has trickled down into business seminars and even some parish programs. Everyone eventually wants to know why they are here and where they are going—good questions that some of us ask too late in life! But the best-selling book of all—the Holy Bible—already tells you what your purpose is: to love God with your whole heart, mind, and soul. Then, filled with His love, your purpose is to love others the way He loves you. Everything else you need and want will flow from that. With a clear purpose of being made in God's image and created to love like He loves, the rest of your life can be built on solid ground.

Your vocation is different than your purpose to love. It's the specific way you live out your life—and where you focus your love—as either single or, married, or as a religious. Many good books have been written on how to discern your vocation. After marriage and divorce, you may need to give some serious thought to your future. Don't just let the time go drifting by. Ask God to give you some clear direction and He will.

Your career is also separate from your purpose. Your job is the way you bring your particular gifts and talents to the community in a way that—hopefully—earns you a decent living.

Your ministry is yet another layer of what you do, but it is not who you are. It is how you bring God's love to the Church and to the world, starting with being a loving and strong parent to your children or a supportive coworker at the office. It can be paid or volunteer—as a prayer partner with others or as a position on a church staff. Do you have a ministry that is separate from your vocation or career?

Let's look at Father Shelton, a Catholic priest.

◇ His purpose in the world is to love God and then others.
◇ His vocation is to the priesthood.
◇ His career is a professor of philosophy at a large university.
◇ His ministry is to serve as campus chaplain.

Your vocation, career, and ministry can change, but your primary purpose—to love—never does. Now let's look at me:

◇ My purpose is to love God and then others. That will never change.
◇ My vocation was to marriage. I knew it

from the time I was a little girl, but in my pride and sinfulness, I blew it by rushing into it foolishly and not making wise and holy choices. For years after my divorce, I discerned with my spiritual director about remaining single, joining a religious order, or attempting a true marriage. Time, prayer, and patience can help to reveal God's will for anyone, including the divorced person.

◇ My career is an author, a speaker, and a producer of Catholic products.

◇ My ministry is to the divorced and anyone whom I can encourage along the way.

These may someday change.

You know your purpose, but what is your vocation, your career, and your ministry? Ask God to help you make those decisions if those decisions still need making.

Your passion

Jeff found his passion and a ministry all in one after his divorce.

I keep busy with things I like to do, not just have to do. One of the best things I've discovered is volunteer work. A friend of mine suggested I join a Doctors Without Borders type group, which I did three years ago. I've since traveled to Central and South America on several medical humanitarian missions, where I translated for US doctors. I also help out several other non-profit groups with their publicity as a volunteer effort. I absolutely love doing this kind of thing. It keeps me busy, and I like using my skills in things that can make a positive difference in the world.

You can, and should, use your passion in your vocation, career, or ministry. As the word *passion* suggests, it is the thing that stir your heart, fires up the imagination, brings you delight and satisfaction, wears you out with a feel-good tiredness, and keeps you so busy you even forget to eat. You can get lost in it, as long as you keep it in order. I have several true passions: writing, solving problems, and cooking a delicious meal and setting a gorgeous table even Martha Stewart would envy! In short, I love to tell stories, fix problems, and bring bounty and beauty to a table for others.

What are your particular passions? Are you finding ways to light the fires, even if they are part-time passions or hobbies? Find them and do them. Then help your children find theirs.

Your personality

Just as God gave you brown eyes or red hair, He gave you the perfect personality to be a unique gift to the world. Your passion definitely arises from your natural temperament—commonly called your personality—which is the part of you that helps you excel and delight in what you do. When I discovered the timeless teachings of the four basic temperaments (often used as a spiritual aid by monks in the middle age), it changed my life. I was able to take off the mask I was wearing to be what others expected and instead be who God made me to be. I also learned to value others' differences instead of sneering, scoffing, or expecting them to change. It is very freeing and really fun. I've written books on the subject, including *Personality Plus at Work*,[1] and teach it in most of my seminars as one of the most powerful tools one can have in improving every relationship—past, present, and with potential new loves.

Your temperament defines how you naturally see and respond to the world around you without stopping to think. Hippocrates—a Greek doctor—coined the four names over three hundred years before Christ. He thought temperaments were in the body fluids, so you may recognize the funny-sounding names. Your natural temperament is your knee-jerk reaction to the world around you. It's your default mode, and it's a combination of two of these four:

The speed and intensity with which you move through life

◇ The *choleric* is task oriented and moves quickly, with a very high energy and intensity, but sometimes overlooks the important and runs over others.

◇ The *phlegmatic* is peaceful and moves more cautiously, thoughtfully, and often more prudently, but may be prone to immobility and can become overwhelmed.

Think Aesop's tortoise and the hare. These two are natural opposites. Even though you may develop some of the traits of both, you are naturally only one.

The lightness or depth in which you see things

◇ The ever-hopeful and sunny *sanguine* is affectionate, light, silly, and quick to forgive but can be too childish and fail to be serious when necessary.

◇ The wary *melancholic* is deep, passionate, sensitive, and creative but can fall into darkness when things are not perfect.

These natural opposites are like oil and water when they do not understand and appreciate each other.

Have you seen yourself or others just in these four

basic descriptions? Each has its own love language that we must learn to speak to build healthy and loving relationships in our vocations, careers, and ministries. While the study of the temperaments is not the only way of looking at personality, most other approaches can find their roots in these four. I hope you'll learn more about them and pass it on to your children. Kids catch on quickly, and they love to know their personalities.

Tools every life shouldn't be without

To rebuild after divorce, especially in the areas of your purpose, passion, and personality, make sure you have these tools in your "garage."

A Catholic Bible—Scripture is God's Holy Word and has so many dimensions we'll never experience them all in this lifetime. But one way of seeing the Bible is that it is a collection of God's love letters to you. It's also a road map to Heaven and blueprints for building a happy and holy life. It's filled with drama, romance, and the greatest adventure of all. If you have a CD player in your car, have the whole family listen to the *Truth and Life*[2] audio dramatized version with top movie stars narrating different parts of the gospels.

The Catechism of the Catholic Church – If you're going to be a Catholic, you'll need to understand what that really means. The *CCC* is a wonderful reference, easy to understand, and is filled with beautiful explanations of why we believe what we believe. It's the official statement of Catholic teaching. Don't take others' words for things—look it up yourself!

At least one good parenting book – We go to ballet classes, soccer lessons, and driver's training, but when we get married, no one requires us to go through a parenting class. Dr. Ray Guarendi (www.DrRay.com) is a Catholic psychologist and the father of ten adopted children, several of whom have special needs. He's smart, funny, and packs a wallop with his parenting advice. You can find his books online or in stores. Some of my other favorites are found in the parenting book section of the Catholic Company (www.catholiccompany.com), and Dr. James Dobson's parenting books are also excellent.

> We go to ballet classes, soccer lessons, and driver's training, but when we get married, no one requires us to go through a parenting class.

A good music collection – Music soothes the savage beast in us all. After divorce, music can especially calm the soul, minister to the melancholy, and lift the spirits. Music is a gift from God that should not be overlooked. Make some time for it.

A good movie collection – Movies are stories that can entertain, distract, lift, and encourage us after divorce. Lose yourself once in a while in a good one. I have a list of suggested movies on our website (www. faithlifeline.com).

A few good cookbooks (or books on other hobbies) – Maybe you don't like to cook, but try it. Forcing yourself to turn off the computer, put away the job list, and escape into the kitchen by yourself or with a friend can be fun—and delicious. There are some easy-to-follow cooking shows on television. Get a few aprons and let the kids try too. Or what about gardening, pottery, collecting, or other healthy hobbies? The list can be endless—but pick a few good ones.

Some good fiction—Jesus taught eternal truths in stories (parables). Wise and holy authors have continued to tell stories that reveal God's truth, His love for us, and the triumph of good over all sorts of evil—including divorce. Adventure, mystery, poetry, history, romance, and even politics are all reflections of being in relationship with God! Good fiction or uplifting poetry can be another fun and fruitful escape when things get just a bit too wound up in your life.

Catholic apologetics – The most important life we can build is what our Church calls the interior life—the life of the soul. The word *apologetics* is not about saying you're sorry you are Catholic; it means being able to give a reason for what you believe. Knowing what the Catholic Church teaches—and why—can give you clarity, insight, and wisdom about not only how to be

Catholic but how to be holy and happy.

A good prayer book – There are countless Catholic prayer books that you can use at certain times of day. Some are ancient and rich; others are newer and light. They all have value if they assist you in prayer. Start perusing Catholic bookstores and get some recommendations or search Catholic Internet sites. And get some good children's prayer books too.

Start small. Get the Bible first. Add to your collection of tools when you hear about something that interests you or your family. And—just as with screwdrivers and saws—encourage your children to begin to use these tools too. You can supervise.

Chapter 23

Gather Around the Fireplace

THEY say that the heart of a home is the kitchen, but I think the fireplace can be a close second. I love to stay with my friend Bonnie in her home in Pennsylvania. I wake up to the smell of fresh-brewed coffee and steaming baked oatmeal, and I make my way downstairs to her cozy kitchen, where there are also the crackling flames and warm glow of a fireplace! Bonnie has the best parts of the house all in one room.

> In rebuilding your life after divorce, it's the flame of God's love that must heat your life and the life of those in your home.

The fireplace is where everyone wants to be—after dinner, on a cold afternoon, or first thing on a chilly morning. In rebuilding your life after divorce, it's the flame of God's love that must heat your life and the life of those in your home. In a certain sense, you want to make your new life, and even your real home, a place where God is remembered, honored, and loved, a true "House of Worship."

Souls ablaze

Fire has always been a symbol of the warmth and intensity of God's love as well as His purification of our hearts, which is evident in the following:

- ◇ God appeared to Moses as a burning bush; the fire consumed the bush but it did not burn. God wants to consume *us* with His love.
- ◇ The Holy Spirit filled the hearts of the apostles at Pentecost by appearing as flames of fire over their heads. He still wants to set *our* hearts ablaze.
- ◇ Jesus said He came to set the world on fire with God's love: "I came to cast fire upon the earth; and would that it were already kindled!" (Luke 12:49). Jesus wants to set *us* on fire too.

Are you familiar with the story and image of Our Lady of Guadalupe? Mary appeared in Mexico in 1531 to Juan Diego, a poor Aztec Indian who had converted to Christianity. She asked him to go to the bishop and instruct him to build a chapel so that people could be converted from their pagan religions. The bishop asked for proof from Juan Diego that the message had indeed come from the Blessed Virgin Mary, and she gave the bishop her image on Juan Diego's cloak. It hangs today in Mexico City, where scientists continue to be baffled by its unexplained mysteries and miraculous properties. One of the things that sets this image apart from others we have of Mary is that she is surrounded by flames and appears to be on fire with love for God. The book of Revelation[1] calls her the "woman clothed with the sun"—who could burn any hotter than that? Mary, help us to burn with love for God as you do!

Basking in the glow of His love

Have you ever sat quietly somewhere and, in a moment of perfect peace, caught the glance of someone you loved? Your eyes lock and no words are spoken, but a lot is being said. What about times when you were hurt or scared and someone you loved gave you a reassuring look—again without words—that said, "I'm here. Don't worry."

This is what Catholics do when they go to Adoration, sitting or kneeling before Jesus in the Blessed Sacrament—the Eucharist—exposed in a beautiful receptacle called a monstrance. There are many ways we can practice the presence of God in our lives at any moment: calling out to Him; seeing Him in nature, another person, music, art, or prayer; and more. But Adoration is different. It is a fuller form of being with God since we believe Jesus, that the Eucharist *is* His true Body and true Blood. Adoration is a quiet time with Him in His Real Presence.

I look at Him and He looks at me

A favorite story of Catholics goes that Saint John Vianney, a French priest known as the Curé of Ars, noticed a poor peasant had been coming to the chapel each day and had stayed for a long time. Curious about the poor man's daily visits, the priest finally asked the fellow what he was doing inside.

"I sit in front of the Blessed Sacrament," was the man's reply.

"And what do you do there?" asked the priest.

The fellow smiled. "I look at Him . . . and He looks at me."

In the peasant's time sitting quietly before our Lord, there were no long litanies of prayers or lists of petitions. There's nothing wrong with formal prayers and petitions, but the man simply sat quietly in the presence of Jesus while they regarded each other in love. This beautiful passage from the *Catechism of the Catholic Church* says more:

Contemplation is a gaze of faith, fixed on Jesus. "I look at him and he looks at me": this is what a certain peasant of Ars in the time of his holy curé used to say while praying before the tabernacle. This focus on Jesus is a renunciation of self. His gaze purifies our heart; the light of the countenance of Jesus illumines the eyes of our heart and teaches us to see everything in the light of his truth and his compassion for all men. Contemplation also turns its gaze on the mysteries of the life of Christ. Thus it learns the "interior knowledge of our Lord," the more to love him and follow him.[2]

Have you ever left work on your lunch hour, gone by the church on your way home, or stopped in on a Saturday afternoon to gaze in love upon the Lord? My mother would sometimes pull into the church parking lot after picking us up from school or running errands and tell us we were all going to "go in for a visit." We'd sit quietly—yes, all of us—and spend time with our Lord in that special way. Why don't you try to give Him ten minutes of alone time this week?

It wouldn't be hard to imagine you are sitting in front of a cozy fireplace when you are before Jesus in the monstrance; it is usually designed in the shape of a golden sunburst, not unlike a crackling fire. Talk to Him. Pour it all out. Sit quietly and listen for a reply. Or simply just sit and be with Him. Nothing has to happen, but sometimes that's when it all happens.

Let His love be the fire in your new life. He loves us without limit and offers Himself to us in the holy Sacrament of the Eucharist. Let Him warm you with His love and purify you with His heat.

Rebuilding tips

Make a time this week to find out what church in your area schedules Adoration. Most church schedules are posted on the Internet.

Visit Jesus. You may feel like offering formal or spontaneous prayers or pouring out your heart, and that's good! But before you leave, practice sitting there quietly and just looking at Him. Let Him look at you.

Make a home altar. Can you find a quiet or separate corner of the house where you can place a picture of Jesus, a Bible, candles, or flowers? Visuals help us move the mind to connect with the love we have for someone, as the family photos on our walls can do. Find some beautiful Catholic art—pictures of Jesus or a simple crucifix—that you like and put them somewhere special. As you pass them throughout the day, they will help you practice the presence of Christ in your new life. And don't forget Mary and your favorite saint too.

Chapter 24

Look Forward to the Best

I NEVER understood Purgatory. Did it really exist? Did you burn there? How long could someone be there? Couldn't you just "pass go" and get straight into Heaven? Understanding purgatory is easier when we bring it back down to earth, as it were. In this last chapter I want to leave you with words of hope and encouragement that there is a rich and satisfying future for you. In a sense, Purgatory is how we know for sure that the best is yet to come.

Preparing for the Bridegroom

You've learned that in the spousal analogy Jesus is the mystical spouse to those who say yes to His proposal. As the hero in our salvation story, He's fought off the dragon of death and goes ahead of us to prepare a heavenly marriage banquet for us for all eternity. In this life, He wants to woo us, wed us, and fill us with divine life. When we leave this earth, He wants to take us home forever. If you've been a bride, you know how thrilling that is! If you've been a bridegroom, you know how exciting is it to carry her over the threshold and present her with all that you have to offer.

But what would you think of the bride who showed up on her wedding day—ready to be carried off to the honeymoon and her new home—in a gorgeous white gown but with bad breath, week-old body odor, greasy hair, and unshaved legs? Ugh! Not pretty. And what an insult to the groom!

That's a perfect picture of what it would be like if the soul went to meet Jesus, the Bridegroom, without first being purified. The white dress represents the state of grace, but the stinky stuff is the unconfessed venial sins, selfish habits, and attachments to things of this world that make us utterly unpresentable to our Love. No one in his right mind would ever want to approach Him in that condition. So we have Purgatory, less of a place than a way we go through "beauty" treatments to make us pure and perfect for our Bridegroom.

Beauty treatments hurt

Guys, you lucked out. You don't have to endure the sting of tweezed eyebrows, the torture of electrolysis to get rid of ugly facial hair, or the burning of acid on your face to reduce wrinkles and sun damage. Since the beginning of time women have suffocated in steam baths, absorbed chemicals into their bodies and hair, and undergone painful and costly procedures—even surgery—to be beautiful for their husbands. It may seem like vanity, and it can be. But it also emerges from the genuine desire of the bride to please her bridegroom. Women were created to bring their special beauty into the world in many unique and creative ways. Since the bride represents all of mankind in the spousal analogy, this desire to be beautiful is also the individual soul's response to Christ. We want to please Him.

You can read about beauty treatments in the romantic and adventurous Old Testament story of Queen Esther. It was an ancient time, and King Ahasuerus ruled over the regions from India to Ethiopia. One day he summoned his queen, Vashti, to join him at a bountiful banquet. The queen was very beautiful but also very uppity. Her regal position had probably gone to her head, and being full of herself, she refused to come when her king called.

It's not nice to say no to the king. The book of Esther tells us "At this the king was enraged, and his anger burned within him." So his wise men advised him to "give her royal position to another who is better than she." Vashti was out; someone else was soon to be in.

Word spread throughout the kingdom, summoning the young women who might be considered suitable for the king. Esther, a young Jewish girl, was among those who came to the palace and was put under the care of Hegai, the royal custodian. Even as beautiful as the girls were, none were to be presented to the king for a full twelve months! First they had to be made presentable to come before him by enduring many beauty treatments. As suggested in a movie version of this biblical story, *One Night with the King*, perhaps Esther and the other girls not only underwent physical procedures but learned etiquette on how to walk, talk, serve, and have pleasing conversation with the king. (A good Catholic prayer life is, indeed, a pleasing conversation with the King!)

Purgatory will hurt too

Now imagine the king is Jesus Christ. In this analogy, physical beauty is a sign of the soul's inner beauty before God. God will search for the soul who wants to accept His proposal and who is willing to do what it takes, for as long as it takes, to present herself suitably before Him. For those who say no to God, they will be out like Vashti. For those who say yes, like Esther, the King will provide the soul's beauty treatments.

In a sense, that's what Purgatory is—the preparation of the soul for Heaven. Even though there really is no time and space (as we know it) after death, we use words like "ten years in Purgatory" to help us understand that some will have to undergo different or deeper purification than others. But the good news is that if you end up in Purgatory, you will see the King. You're already on palace grounds! There's a wait and painful "procedures" as sin and attachments are plucked and shaved from us. But this time of purgation and pain is mixed with the sweet consolation that Heaven is right around the corner. The best is yet to come.

Our life on earth is also preparatory

Queen Esther's year in preparation is also a picture of our time on earth before we go to meet the King in Heaven. Life—and especially divorce—has a way of buffering, bleaching, plucking, burning, and stinging us. What will we do with those painful periods? Let them make us bitter . . . or better?

The Church teaches that suffering can actually be one of those painful treatments that make us much more beautiful in the end. Just like the bride who may not look forward to the painful plucking or the sting of undergo-

> All of life is about our uniting intimately with the Bridegroom—even on His Cross.

ing a hot wax treatment, she understands it can have a desirable result and submits herself to it out of love for her bridegroom. The Church calls it redemptive suffering, and it can be a way of our knowing, even through suffering, the best is yet to come.

All of life is about our uniting intimately with the Bridegroom—even on His Cross. Our suffering after divorce can have great meaning and power as long as we don't waste it on anger and self pity. It works like this:

From the Cross, Jesus' suffering and death became the living fountain of all graces—including our eternal salvation. That fountain of grace flows beyond time and space and is available for drinking deeply by every generation for all time.

Your suffering also flows from you, like blood, and you can let it spill into the ground where it pools and coagulates, dries up, and does nothing. Or you can (through an act of the will) unite your pain into the same river of redemption that flows from Jesus' side. The blood and water that flow from *your* heart can mingle with *His* and be changed to a source of healing and grace for you and others. From that intimate union of blood comes new life.

Just as a bride freely offers her body to her bridegroom on their wedding night, when we offer Christ our own sufferings, He receives them and impregnates them with the power of divine life. He uses your anguish, mixed with His, to bring about life, love, and healing to others—even the salvation of souls.

Waiting for the best

Once you're established in your new life after a civil divorce, you'll notice two things: Even though you may be healed, there will still be crosses to bear, and your heart will always be restless until it rests in Him.

I hope you'll keep a balanced view between loving this life and longing for your true home in Heaven. It will help you keep proper perspective when the next set of problems comes. And remember, a little bit of Heaven is not totally unattainable in this life. We can taste the heavenly banquet when we choose to unite our hearts with Christ, especially at the sacrifice of the Mass. Father Vincent Serpa, OP, wrote in the Catholic Answers online forum recently:

> Your [spouse] may have left you, but He has not. . . . Whenever He allows obstacles to fall in our life's path, He is inviting us to share His Cross. This means that He wants us to come closer. He wants us closer to Himself. He wants more of our attention. He wants our company.[1] God wants *your* company. He loves you so much.

Epilogue

The Best Is Yet to Come

WHEN I started writing this book I'd been divorced and alone for what seemed forever. I've had some good times and lots of blessings, but it has also been a painful and purifying process. I've had to relearn who God is, how deeply Christ loves me, what it means to be a woman and to be Catholic, and how to love the right way. I've fallen, been depressed and on meds, cried, felt desperate, gone to confession, thrown myself at His mercy, and gotten back up again. But He has never left me—even when it felt like He had.

One night, years ago, I was driving home from a day trip to Los Angeles through the lonely, dark desert night on Interstate 10 in the Southern California desert. I was particularly depressed, somewhat distracted and on autopilot, and hoping to get home soon. Suddenly I felt a keen sense of God's presence, and these words went through my head, *Look out the window to your right. Right now.* Having learned to listen and follow those inner promptings, I quickly looked away from the road to a lone billboard stuck in the desert sand. As the car whizzed past at seventy miles an hour, I barely was able to read the large white letters on the solid black background: THE BEST IS YET TO COME. Nothing else. No pictures and no other words.

Whoa, I thought. *Is that You talking to me? Okay, okay, I hear You loud and clear. I'll quit feeling sorry for myself and trust You. Thank You.* That was almost fourteen years ago, and I've never forgotten His message to me. But something else quite mysterious happened more recently.

In October 2009 I attended a joint fortieth reunion of several Catholic high schools in Sacramento, California. As I plucked and tweezed and shaved to look beautiful that night, I thought of my old senior-year sweetheart, Bob. I'd gone to the Catholic girls' school, he to the all-boys Jesuit school down the street. We'd dated all year long and then broke up when we both went away to different colleges. I wondered whether he might be there and what he might look like. I found out when I walked in and saw him sitting at the bar.

His face lit up in a smile when he saw me, and my stomach immediately turned to jelly. I tried to be cool, calm, and collected, but I think he knew I was feeling the same excitement as he was. Could there be a possibility of love after all this time? If so, I knew this time it had to be the way that Christ and the Church had shown me. I could never again attempt romance and marriage in any other way than what God has always desired for all of us. We talked, and right away I threw out that I was devoted to my faith and happy to be Catholic. He didn't balk. He was open and revealing about himself too, and there was something sweet and promising that we both decided to further pursue. I was scared but excited about the possibilities. I thanked him, we hugged, and I left early to drive home the next day to Southern California.

When I got home, I found that he'd sent pink roses, and he started calling me every night. Two weeks later he flew down to visit, and I decided to take him on a tour of the Palm Springs area. I thought I'd start with some of the natural desert sights and end up downtown at some kitschy local joints. On our way I thought it would be fun to pop into the Palm Springs cemetery where Frank Sinatra and other famous movie stars are buried. I'd never been there, but I'd heard people traditionally would leave pennies on Frank's headstone. I was eager for Bob's arrival, but the chatter inside my head was all about promising God that I would do things right this time. And I meant it!

I picked him up at the airport, and we drove out to the Salton Sea and back, laughing, connecting, and having a wonderful day. On our way into Palm Springs, we drove into the cemetery. We got out of the car, walked across the grass to the small headstone, and found the name Frances Albert Sinatra. I caught my breath when I read the simple inscription: THE BEST IS YET TO COME. Was God speaking again?

Over dinner that night I shared my billboard story with my old flame, and our affection for each other—and our hope—ignited. Despite our past failures, we set out together on a path we'd never taken: following God's blueprints—not our own—for building a real marriage. There were more dates, long talks, big arguments, and making up, and I found myself in a true courtship.

Finally he proposed, I said yes, and we got all of our civil and Church paperwork in order. On the Thursday afternoon of June 23, 2011, my high-school sweetheart and I went to the Sacrament of Reconciliation together in preparation for the Sacrament of Matrimony the next day, where we exchanged Catholic wedding vows, witnessed in the church by Father Healy. Because we'd followed Church teaching and saved sex for our wedding night, my new husband laughed nervously about our honeymoon. "I feel like a kid again—just like when I met you. I'm not sure I'll know what to do!" I giggled and gave him a tender squeeze; I felt the same way. We *were* like teenagers again! The next three days in California's exquisite Napa Valley wine country was a sweet and tender time for us both, with purity of mind and heart restored by God's graces.

As I finish this book, I have to pinch myself! I'm married. Gulp! I'm closer to old age than middle age, and I've moved five hundred miles to the San Francisco Bay area from the desert. I tore up deep roots and left my business, relatives, friends, beautician, doctor, dentist, neighbors, and church family to start a new life with Bob. Because it would be ridiculous to have two living room sofas and two toasters, I trashed, sold, or donated almost everything I owned. Some days I am still in shock—but give me time.

Bob and I are building a home with our foundation in Christ. Sure, the roof leaks every once in a while, and we don't always keep our closets clean. But there are no secrets in the cellar, and life is good. I believe it's because we both know that it is not marriage that makes man happy—it's God. The heart of God is our *true* home. We know that the joys in our lives pale in comparison with the joys of eternal life.

The hope you and I have is real. I want you to believe (even if it feels hopeless sometimes) that the best is yet to come for you too. That is the promise we have as Christians.

I asked the divorced men and women I interviewed to give some last words of encouragement to my readers:

⋄ Be open and listen to the Holy Spirit when He talks to you. For me, it's the little voice that comes from somewhere inside.

⋄ Turn inward; heal with God, or no relationship will work.

◇ Make God the center of your life. Love Him, and everything else will fall into place.

And since I have let Jeff close a few other chapters, he can close this one as well. Thanks, Jeff.

The thought I think recent divorcees need to keep in mind is this: Your life isn't ending. It could be just beginning. Embrace it. It's full of new possibilities of good things, and there will be happiness in your life again. And what I'm finding now, nearly six years after my divorce, is that the life that I once thought was ending is really just beginning. And just when we think the curtain is about to come crashing down on us, the curtain goes up again and we're thrust into a new scene. When the storm passes, you may realize what I realized—the best is yet to come.

—Jeff

Notes

Introduction

[1] Isaiah. 53:3
[2] Sweet, Rose. *A Woman's Guide to Healing the Heartbreak of Divorce.* Peabody: Hendrickson Publishers, 2001.
[3] Sweet, Rose. *Healing the Divorced Heart.* Chattanooga: AMG Publishers, 2003.

Chapter 4— Let God Lead You

[1] DeMille, C. (Director). (1956). *The Ten Commandments* [Motion picture]. United States: Paramount.

Chapter 6—Enjoy Making Plans

[1] Sweet, Rose. *Dear God, Send Me a Soul Mate.* Chattanooga: AMG Publishers, 2002.

Chapter 9—Expect an Adequate Timeframe

[1] Smolowe, Jill. "Disaster in Japan: Tragedy and Hope." *People,* March 28, 2011.

Chapter 11—Clear Your Title

1 Sweet, Rose. *Understanding and Petitioning for Your Decree of Nullity*. Charlotte: Saint Benedict Press, 2011.
2 Hebrews 13:5
3 Matthew 19:26

Chapter 12—Erect Sturdy Boundaries

1 Matthew 12:33
2 Evert, Jason, Crystalina Evert, and Brian Butler. *Theology of the Body for Teens*. West Chester: Ascension Press, 2006.
3 Pinto, Matthew. *Freedom: Twelve Lives Transformed by Theology of the Body*. West Chester: Ascension Press, 2009.

Chapter 14—Clear Out Your Closets

1 Benet, Lorenzo, "Heroes Among Us." *People*, February 28, 2011.

Chapter 15—Stock Up Your Kitchen

1 John 6:51

Chapter 17—Keep Up on Your Cleaning

1 Sweet, Rose. *Healing the Divorced Heart*. Chattanooga: AMG Publishers, 2003.

Chapter 18—Don't Hide Things in the Cellar

1 West, Christopher. *Theology of the Body Explained*. Boston: Pauline Books and Media, 2007, 235.

Chapter 19—Learn to Love Your Laundry Room

1 1 John 5:16
2 Donovan, Colin B. Eternal Word Television Network (EWTN), accessed October 13, 2011, http://www.ewtn.com/expert/answers/mortal_versus_venial.htm.

Chapter 22—Equip Your Garage

1 Littauer, Florence and Rose Sweet. *Personality Plus at Work*. Grand Rapids: Revell, 2011.
2 *Truth and Life Dramatized Audio Bible*. Grand Rapids: Zondervan, 2010.

Chapter 23—Gather Around the Fireplace

1 Apocalypse 12:1
2 *Catechism of the Catholic Church*, paragraph 2715.

Chapter 24—Look Forward to the Best

1 "What can a husband do if marriage fails?" Catholic Answers forum, accessed October 13, 2011, http://forums.catholic.com/showthread.php?t=517754.

ℐlso available from Rose Sweet . . .

ℐou CAN understand annulment—you just need a little help!

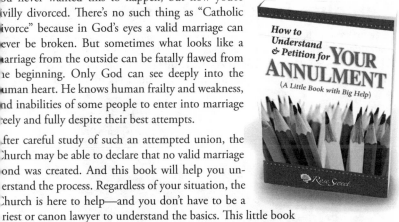

ou never wanted this to happen, but now you're ivilly divorced. There's no such thing as "Catholic ivorce" because in God's eyes a valid marriage can ever be broken. But sometimes what looks like a aarriage from the outside can be fatally flawed from ae beginning. Only God can see deeply into the uman heart. He knows human frailty and weakness, nd inabilities of some people to enter into marriage eely and fully despite their best attempts.

fter careful study of such an attempted union, the Church may be able to declare that no valid marriage ond was created. And this book will help you un-erstand the process. Regardless of your situation, the Church is here to help—and you don't have to be a riest or canon lawyer to understand the basics. This little book vith big help dispels the common myths and misunderstandings about marriage, di-orce, and annulments, and is helpful for:

Divorced men and women who are considering if they have grounds for an annulment
Those who need help completing their formal petition for a Decree of Nullity (annulment)
Lay or religious ministers who work with the separated and divorced
Parish priests and deacons involved in divorce ministry
Those who counsel divorced Catholics
Anyone who wants to know more about what the Church really teaches about divorce

> *I was afraid of the annulment process at first, but found it incredibly healing and even freeing. I learned so much about myself and was able to forgive my ex-spouse—and ask for forgiveness as well.*
> *– Patty*

> *I had no idea of what the Church really taught about marriage and divorce. I thought I did, but I was blown away when I learned the truth. Going through the annulment process actually made me hunger to know more of my Catholic faith. – Jim*

Price: $12.95

SBN: 9781935302605

To order visit SaintBenedictPress.com or call 800.437.5876

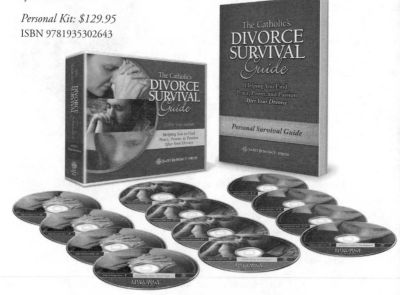